To my favourite Things… The colouring-in department, Miss small person and Master small person xxx

CONTENTS

FOREWORD

We all know when we meet someone who is doing their Thing. They are more interesting. More engaging. They wave their hands about more when they talk. They are more passionate – about work, about life, about everything. And generally speaking, they are better at what they do. They know more about it. They have thought more about it. The world is a better place because of all these things.

Lucy Whittington is definitely someone who is 'doing her Thing'. When you hear her speak for the first time you know there is something different. Something resonates. You know what she is saying is true, even though you might not have heard it expressed precisely like this before. It catches something inside you and you begin to see possibilities you hadn't seen before. Her vision is a world where everyone is doing their Thing. Her Thing is helping that happen, one person at a time.

As she speaks, that world unfolds before us. Imagine if everyone you interacted with had that same glow of passion around them. Plumbers, doctors, artists, teachers. We've all met some of these, and we all know the difference. Sometimes they appear in unexpected places: the school caretaker who greets everyone he meets with a cheerful smile and 'hello'; the gardener who wants to talk at length about plans and designs and progress every time you walk past – whether it's your own garden they are working on, or an unrelated garden five doors up the street; the shoe shop owner who goes to great lengths to get you the right fit, and explains it all in detail, and the shoes they finally sell you feel like you were born with them on your feet…

Imagine if everyone you met had similar passion for their work. Everything would be done well. There would be no customer complaints departments, and all the unhappy people who work in them could be recycled back into the workforce, ready to find and do their Thing; customer service would be a totally different world, a place where supporting the customer joyfully would be rewarding work for the people whose Thing that is.

In a world of everyone doing their Thing, everything would work. Inanimate objects would do what they are supposed to do, when they are supposed to do them – can openers and air conditioning systems and mobile phone networks – because the people who design them and the people who make them would be focused and creative and innovative, filled with the energizing joy of doing their Thing.

I could go on, but you get the point. So how do we create this Utopian world? Where do we start? It starts with you. Are you doing your Thing? In your work, in your family, with your friends, in your life? It's probably a question you know the answer to without having to think much about it. It might be 'yes' – in which case, brilliant! This book will help you take that further, do it bigger and brighter, get it further out into the world, benefiting more people. It might be 'no' – in which case this book will help you find your Thing, develop it and start doing it for the benefit of yourself and others.

Once you are doing your Thing, you stand out like a beacon. That's the spotlight that Lucy talks about. It's magnetic and exciting and it inspires others to do the same.

I've been impatient to see this book complete. Online, in person, on the radio, in interviews and on stage, Lucy has been sharing this message with many, many people. I want her to reach more. This thing is like a snowball. As one person reaches inside them and makes the bold move to step into their Thing, the standard rises. Once we've experienced the exceptional, we begin to expect it, and it becomes the new norm. That's what I want. I want everyone I interact with to wear the smile of someone who is totally fulfilled in their work. I want you to read this book and raise your standard – not in 'professionalism' or 'quality' but in inspiration, the wild flow of life pouring through you.

That's what doing your Thing makes possible.

Read this book. Let your mind run as ideas pop up. Stop and make notes. Put the ideas into practice. Take some bold, brave steps. Then once you've done that, look around to see where people you know are doing this and congratulate them, thank them. Let them know you see it and appreciate it and want them to keep doing it. Then look around again and see where people are not doing their Thing, or not to the full. You know they have passions and skills and talents but they aren't being used to the extent they could be. Encourage them, gently, tactfully; or boldly and rudely, to make some changes. And give them a copy of this book.

Don't we all want it? That world full of people – everyone – doing their Thing?

Thanks, Lucy. You've changed countless lives already. You've changed mine. Thank you – a BIG, BIG thank you – for doing your Thing.

Jennifer Manson – The Flow Writer – doing my Thing.

INTRODUCTION

You know when someone has found their Thing – they have that annoying 'I can't believe I get paid for doing something easy that I love' look of smugness and wonder about them. Like when you see famous actors interviewed who can't quite believe their luck that they get paid millions to dress up and enjoy themselves for a few weeks when making a movie. Or when you see a super-successful author hit the jackpot just from doing what they love (J.K. Rowling springs to mind).

My Thing is absolutely what I love to do. My Thing is that I help people find *their* Thing. More specifically, I help people find their Thing and then get famous for it. My intention in this book (and everywhere I do my Thing) is to create the space for people to find that Thing they are brilliant at and then help them get paid for it. It's like marketing meets business strategy meets personal branding with a few Lucy sparkles on top.

Until I did it, I'd always known I wasn't doing my Thing. Don't get me wrong, I was very good at what I did (and that was a lot of things), it's just that I wasn't doing MY Thing. It's hard to put your finger on it but if you know, you know. I can stand up in front of a room of people and say 'I help people find their Thing' and anyone in the room who hasn't found their Thing yet gets it immediately. They know. Just like you knew – which is why I'm guessing you're reading this book. I'm guessing you've not quite nailed it yet (your Thing that is).

This doesn't necessarily mean you're drifting around right now in the middle of an 'I'm trying to find myself' gap year (although it might be, and that's okay!). It's just that nag, that doubt, or if it's been there a while, that SHOUTING that is telling you 'this' isn't it. This is just some-thing, not your THING thing. After all, was this REALLY what you were born to do? Just be 'good' at something? Very often 'this' is a job you're doing when you actually want to be doing your own thing instead. But if you're going to take that leap into working for yourself you want it to be your 'Thing' thing otherwise you may as well stick where you are, doing another thing for someone else! Or maybe you took the leap already – you have a business, or you're a consultant selling something you're good at – but it's not your Thing thing and you know it. Maybe you're just doing what you're 'good' at to pay the bills and it's not exciting you…

What I do is find that Thing you do that's brilliant. And I didn't know this was MY Thing until I started looking for it. And I started looking for it because I'd gotten grumpy.

Why being grumpy is great

The typical side-effect of not doing your Thing yet is that you are grumpy about what you are doing. But this is good. If you're grumpy, you're far more likely to do something about how you feel than if you're 'okay'. I do also help people who are 'okay' but want more, but it's when the grumpy kicks in that more of the motivation to change does too. So yes, I like grumpy people!

I once had someone message me (on Facebook, where all good business is done!) to say he was 'beyond annoyed' that he didn't know his Thing yet (yes Dave that was you!). That was grumpy kicking in… ☺ and let's just say that he's doing his Thing now because when you KNOW you're not doing it, the next step is to be open to what you're already doing that's brilliant (plenty more on that to come). It can be easy to find, but you need to know where to look and what to do with it when you find it.

Good news – you already have it

The good thing about your Thing is that you already have it. Everything you've done up to now, everything you've learnt, watched, read, experienced, understood, formed an opinion on, worked out a better way for, reacted to, adapted to, challenged, accepted and said – all of that is your Thing. Because when it comes down to it, your Thing is YOUR thing. It's what YOU do that's brilliant and it's entirely yours to own. No-one else's Thing is exactly like yours. No-one's. And that's a really good thing when it comes to selling it, as everyone wants to buy something that's different.

So, while I can help you 'find' your Thing, it's not actually lost. A bit like when you run around the house barking 'where are my sunglasses?' and you realise they've been on top of your head the entire time and, of course, everyone else could see them as plain as day… hmm, yes that's the Thing's best hiding place – in plain sight of everyone else (more on that later). The good news that you already have your Thing means there's no new qualification to pass or item to buy to get it. The trick lies in seeing it and then doing something with it! And in my world, doing something with your Thing means getting paid for it.

Here's what's coming…

This book will take you through the process I have used over and over to help people just like you find their Thing. I'll tell you where to look for your Thing and what it will feel like when you have it – those are the 'Finding Your Thing' chapters in Part One. Then I'll suggest (strongly!) what to do with your Thing once you've got it – that's the 'Getting Famous for Your Thing' chapters in Part Two. I am pretty serious when it comes to Things as the last thing I want you to do is find it then stuff it away in a cupboard out of sight so no-one gets the benefit of it. Don't get me started on that... When you have your Thing my recommendation is that you get 'business famous' for it. You learn how to sell your brilliant Thing to the people who need it.

Now of course once you know your Thing you can go and find a job doing it. And in fact, I do have some clients who – once they'd found their Thing – were able to find a job description that fitted, or were able to 'develop' their current role to do their Thing. Corrine was determined to work independently as a coach but when she saw her Thing was helping people manage choices she saw opportunities in her job (as a Business Analyst) to coach there. Having said that, Corrine has since taken the leap and is 'on her own', so don't rule out going solo. For most people though (and definitely myself), it's not an option to find a job doing your Thing. If you ask me, the best way to really do your Thing is to do it YOUR way.

Being an Indie Professional

'Indie Professional' is the name I've given to those people who are best doing their Thing (and getting paid for it). These are the people I absolutely love and choose to work with. It means being business-like, being different and definitely doing your Thing your way. It's important to me that it's 'Indie' not plain old 'independent'. Why be normal when you can do something brand new?

Being an Indie Professional means you're in charge – it's *your* business that's allowing you to do your Thing, get paid for it and then get business famous for it. And who wouldn't want that?

Getting business famous

To make your business easy, my advice is to get known and sought after for your Thing. Just like being 'properly' famous, you'll be well known and recognised but the difference in being a 'Business Celebrity' is that what you're known for is a valuable business service or product (not that I'm suggesting all celebrities are air-heads or anything… there's the odd exception, right? ☺).

Valuing your Thing means you'll get paid for doing your Thing. And if you can get paid for doing your Thing then you've just reached that holy grail of 'doing what you love' for your work. So now we're talking: life purpose, fulfillment, legacy – or just smiling every day, that works too.

So here's what being business famous looks like: you, standing in your own spotlight, clearly showing off what you do that's brilliant – so your value is clear and obvious to those who need it. It's about confidently attracting attention, not desperately seeking it. It's about being bold and being in business, not simply shouting and showing off with nothing to share (see previous comment about vacuous celebrities!).

The fact that you get paid for doing your Thing also demonstrates the value of what you know and have experienced. Build a business around this and you'll have something that's exciting, easy and yours. You'll have created a mini monopoly and that means you can charge and supply exactly what you want to. And while a monopoly is definitely not a good thing when it's a utility company it's brilliant when it's your business. Welcome to being in charge.

It's on the end of your nose

You could stop reading now because I've just told you exactly where your Thing is! We're not even done with the Introduction and already I'm giving it all away...

> **Your Thing is on the end of your nose**

Think about that – it's right there, plain as day in the middle of your face. Everyone else can see it. You can see everyone else's too. But yours? Nope. No chance, not even if you go cross-eyed. If you want to see the end of your own nose you'll need a mirror. And that's my intention as you read on – keep looking for yourself reflected in the stories and examples of how things show up, so you start to see your own Thing.

You're looking straight past it

Because your Thing is on the end of your nose, it means you look straight past it every day... your Thing is so 'there' it's not there. You overlook it, stare right past it and just get on with what needs doing. You look past what you do brilliantly. Everything that's automatic and natural for you is actually your Thing... but you don't see its value, you just do it.

But surely that's just common sense? Sure it is. It's common sense to you because it's *your* Thing... But your common sense isn't someone else's common sense. So it's actually uncommon sense.

Am I making sense? Keep reading and all will be revealed. Thing finding this way…

How to use this book

If you're a fast reader like me you might want to race through this book in one go, and please do (after all, I want you to read it!). But I also encourage you to pause and ponder while you do. You will never find your Thing by looking 'really hard' for it; instead, it shows up in the spaces you leave. So however you need to create space, do it – take a break, look out of the window for a few minutes or write a few notes while you have a cup of tea, whatever works for you.

The book takes you through a process, so the order does make a difference. Of course you can skip to the chapter that takes your fancy, but the ideas build up as you read through so bear that in mind… And while it's been written in order, this isn't one of those 'and here's another exercise you must do now – fill in the blanks before you go on to the next step' books. They annoy me, as I just want to read on and find out what's next! But that's not to say I don't suggest you do some of the exercises, or work some ideas through, just do them when you want to.

I've left a few pages at the back of the book if you need to scribble down thoughts and ideas (although I'd prefer you did that in pencil as I'm one of those 'don't bend the spine, books are sacred' kind of people!). ☺ And of course if you're reading this on a Kindle, you can just stare at those blank pages and meditate! Take your time, enjoy and let your Thing show up in the spaces.

PART ONE

FINDING YOUR THING

Chapter 1

WHY FIND YOUR THING?

I could answer with 'why not?' Do you want to always just do what you're good at or would you like to do what you're brilliant at instead? That's the difference between doing your Thing and not. Would you like easy work or hard work? Would you like to leave a legacy or just leave? Doing your Thing is about sharing your gift – and you can take that in a 'talent' or 'life purpose' way or you can merely think about it as the type of gift that you wrap and present to someone. If you were able to give the perfect gift to someone – maybe it's an answer, or an idea, a different way of thinking, a product that solves a problem or just an angle that works better – what would you give? You have something that will be the perfect 'gift' for someone else but chances are you've not wrapped it up and handed it over yet. And just as a side note, I'd be charging for this gift not giving it away.

Here's my Thing

It's going to make sense for me to tell you a bit about me and my Thing so you can see how it works and relate it back to where you are. Now I'll be honest, there was a time when I thought my Thing would be more 'Kylie' or 'Kate Moss' than it ended up being. Clearly I am neither an international pop star nor a world-famous supermodel; it turns out my Thing is something else.

I've always loved business and the way it 'works'. My first degree was in Economics (joint honours with Politics for my sins!), so clearly this was never going to lead me to international pop stardom. That said, it's clearly not led me to being Chancellor of the Exchequer either. I've also, in the pursuit of thinking my Thing lay in qualifications, got an MBA too. Like I said I love business, but this extra 3-year studying stint was perhaps taking things too far. Oh and then there's the MCIM too (Member of the Chartered Institute of Marketing). Yes it's true, I was a letters-after-my-name collector for a time, which is actually all part of looking for my Thing with hindsight, because I figured when I got that perfect qualification I'd feel I'd got 'there'.

If you already run your own business I'm sure you'll agree that the best way to learn about business is to have one. There's only so far 'theory' can take you, the rest you need to work out as you go along 'for real'. The irony of course is that I worked in marketing for most of the time I had a 'proper job' but you only really 'get' marketing when you have to sell yourself. Ha, if only I'd known…

So I worked my way up from Marketing Assistant to Marketing Director, taking in small start-ups and international plcs along the way, and 'found' myself an 'expert' in business software marketing. Has this happened to you? Expertise 'finds' you even though you maybe didn't choose it – just because you hang around long enough doing something. Now business software marketing might sound a little bit exciting but when I spell out that actually I was marketing accounting and payroll software I am sure any ideas you have of excitement will soon disappear (don't worry, I'm used to it!).

So, while I maybe hadn't chosen this 'Thing', I still saw it as valuable and when I started my own business in 2005 I carried on doing what I was known for. Yes I did the lazy thing – I did my old 'job' as a consultant and worked in the business software industry doing marketing. Hardly the 'big leap' into the unknown as a risk-taking entrepreneur, instead I merely went independent. That said, I got paid more, I was in charge of my own time and if I wanted to I could work in my pyjamas. ☺ This was me being an 'Independent Professional' but not an 'Indie Professional'. It's easy to mistake doing a thing for your Thing thing. But you'll know if it isn't your Thing, as it just won't sit perfectly with you. I knew I was just doing something to get paid.

And so it continued. I carried on doing what I was 'good' at, because after all I'd be daft to do anything else… I was getting paid… I had referrals… this was easy… But I knew. I knew it wasn't my Thing. I knew this wasn't what I was here to do. It wasn't big enough. So I thought about it (a lot), and decided that I could choose something else. I decided I had to go shopping to find something that fitted me perfectly, instead of just wearing what I'd been given.

And so I went to the niche supermarket

Before you get excited and ask me for directions, this is not a real shop it's a metaphor. I'd always been looking for that 'perfect fit'. If you've had even a whiff of marketing theory cross your path you'll know that having a niche is considered to be nirvana. Without a niche in your business, life is not worth living, etc. It's not quite that drastic but it is super-helpful to have a niche not just from a marketing perspective but from a doing something you actually like perspective too. If you specialise it's a lot easier to get noticed and known than if you're a generalist. Same thing with musicians, artists and the like – they pick a niche or genre to get famous more easily.

So, I cast aside all assumptions that I had no experience in certain markets and just picked out from the shelf the nicest-looking niche I could see. (This is the way you shop, right? You don't get the store to design your perfect niche, you just buy the best one they have.) The niche supermarket is FULL of niches, so like a savvy shopper you find the one that you like the most and buy it.

Here's how the equation works (in theory):

Thing You Love	+	What You're Good At	=	Perfect Niche & Business Nirvana

For me this looked like:

I love travel and hotels marketing	+	I am good at marketing	=	Travel & hotel

This is, of course, highly logical and makes perfect sense. And I was excited because I 'chose' this (instead of my expertise choosing for me just from doing it for long enough!). Because when I say I love travel and hotels I mean I am OBSESSED. I know everyone likes a holiday but *Condé Nast Traveller* magazine is my porn. So this niche made total sense. Given the choice of any industry to grace my marketing talents with, it made sense to pick a market I loved. And that's what looked good to me in the niche supermarket, so I bought it…

Next, I did what I know how to do. I wrote the book (*Hotel Success Handbook* if you want to look it up – I think it's still no. 1 on Amazon for Hotel Marketing). I networked, I tweeted, I wrote the free report, I showed up, I got noticed, I got clients – as after all, I am good at marketing. There was a problem though. I just wasn't excited. How could it be my Thing if I wasn't excited? Because I would be excited if I was doing my Thing. Hmm…

It's like dating…

Finding your Thing is very much like dating. You cannot rely 100% on logic; your heart has to come into the equation somewhere. Now excuse me if I work from theory and somewhat hazy memory here as I've been married for a long time ☺ but you know there's the people who 'look perfect on paper' – they 'tick all the boxes' on your perfect partner check list and yet… you turn up to the date and even though they are 'perfect'…

You

Just

Don't

Fancy

Them

And that's what can happen when you 'pick a niche' from the niche supermarket instead of finding your Thing. Of course you pick the best available but it can easily not be quite right – you're not in love with it. The world of online dating profiles is very much like a niche supermarket – that list of features might make sense but if the spark isn't there then it's not going to happen.

In fact, let's be honest, sometimes the person you do date often has 'essentials' missing from the check list… And that's just like what happened to me when I followed the formula to find my niche. I came up with a business that seemed 'perfect on paper' but it was NOT the one where I was doing my Thing. It's never a good idea to use a 'check list' for matters of the heart (I'd still be looking for a husband for a start I'm sure!) so be open to other options… they are probably right in front of you (he was).

The two types

The problem was, I had forgotten that there are two types of business owners. Type 1 has a business because they don't want a job or a boss. Totally commendable and understandable, however this rarely makes a risk taker when it comes to marketing (or anything else). Type 2 has a business because it's an expression of who they are. It's the work they have to do, it's what they want to share with the world, it's their art. These are the entrepreneurs, Indie Professionals and risk takers. They will do their Thing because they have to do their Thing. And I realised: I only like working with Type 2.

It turns out that not many of the people who own hotels or run travel companies are Type 2… except that's not always obvious 'on paper'. I needed to go on lots of 'dates' to find that out!

Meanwhile, out learning…

All this time I was not doing my Thing thing I was still attending seminars and workshops, listening to marketing and business speakers and generally 'learning' my head off as that's what I like to do. I'd be meeting brilliant business owners and engaging entrepreneurs at these events and they'd be saying things like 'Oh

I wish I could get more clients' or 'If only more people knew about me' or 'I just want marketing that works' or 'I hate marketing' (!) or 'I don't know how to stand out', usually alongside 'So many people do what I do', etc.

To me it was obvious

Every person I met who was 'complaining' had one obvious thing missing in their business – them. There was no personality in their marketing and message. It was wall-to-wall 'brochure speak' – too much 'we' and not enough 'why'. There weren't enough stories – no-one was taking a real stand for what they believed in and knew. They weren't communicating and telling us their point of view. They were wondering why they didn't have clients when all the while they sounded just like everyone else. It was obvious to me… They weren't telling us about their Thing. Their market couldn't see that brilliant Thing they did that only they did, so they got lumped in with 'everyone else' and were lost.

So why wasn't anyone telling them?

It was so glaringly obvious to me that it couldn't possibly be 'just' this that was holding people back? Surely? It was so simple and so obvious – total common sense in fact. There was absolutely no reason (in my mind) why these fabulous entrepreneurs and business owners couldn't have tons of clients knocking at their door. After all, they were brilliant at what they did. They all had a great Thing, they just weren't telling anyone about it. Oh hang on a minute. That was the problem! They didn't see it. They literally couldn't see what was on the end of their own nose. But that's okay, I thought – someone will point it out to them. Someone else will do that…

So I waited.

And I waited.

Surely someone else would say it.

Surely someone else who was more qualified/smarter/more established/better looking... would tell them their Thing. I mean, it was SO obvious. They may as well have had neon signs blinking 'I'm not telling people about my Thing' above their heads. But apparently it was not obvious to everyone. No-one was telling them.

Turns out that someone was me

Now I'll be honest, it took me a while to realise it was me who should be saying something. It took me MONTHS to realise that no-one had actually pointed out the obvious. No-one had told these people they had a Thing, or to go 'get famous' for their Thing or even work out what their Thing was in the first place. Which was odd. It was so obvious to me that surely there were plenty of people 'out there' who saw it too. There were those neon signs after all! There must be plenty of people more qualified than me who saw Things. And that's why I waited. I'd bump into the same people at events and online. Again and again. It finally dawned on me, if no-one else was telling them, maybe I should. But there was a problem...

I'd niched myself into a corner

Remember that trip to the niche supermarket? When I'd picked travel and hotel marketing off the shelf because it looked nice? Well of course that was a problem. I couldn't actually help anyone unless they owned a hotel or a travel company as that was my business now. And that started to annoy me. A lot. I got very grumpy. But GRUMPY leads to GREATNESS. I've mentioned that already. And so I knew I had to do something about this grumpy. I had to help the people I was meeting no matter what their business or market and tell them what I saw, **throws travel and hotel niche out the window**.

Being a Business Celebrity was born. My new business would be all about showing people how to get famous for what they do that's brilliant. In fact, my very first strapline was 'Find out what it takes to get noticed in your market'.

Now I say my business was born but at first it was only an idea and then I freaked out. After all, who the hell was I to tell anyone how to be a Business Celebrity?! That's most certainly a WTF moment – filed next to 'Are you insane?' – because while I was maybe 'famous' in a tiny way to a few people in business, I wasn't exactly Richard Branson. So I panicked and shelved it. Not on a high enough shelf though…

On a shelf, not quite out of reach

This is where a lot of people put their Thing once they find it. They don't DO it, they just place it on a shelf not quite out of reach – so they can (in theory) grab it and start doing it right away. But in practice they just keep an eye on it on that shelf, not quite out of sight; they have it 'taunt' them until they are 'beyond annoyed' and they have to take it down and do something with it.

A lot of Indie Professionals I work with have been working on their 'indie' ideas for some time – very often certifying as coaches 'on the side' of their jobs, or getting qualified in a 'hobby' so that they can now teach (yoga is very popular!). Lots of personal development/business seminars are attended and their Amazon account has shipped a lot of books… ☺ So while the idea of putting all this new learning into practice as part of their Thing is right and they KNOW it's all part of their Thing, it doesn't always 'make sense' and is very often not a safe option.

A safe option is a job promotion, not self-promotion of a brand new Thing – that's scary and unknown! And while for some people brand new means excitement, for many others it's sheer terror – and those people are the shelvers! Their Thing will stay on the shelf until it 'makes sense' (they think), which very rarely happens – instead it just gets too distracting to ignore any more… ☺

After a few months of oscillating between shall I, shan't I? Can I, can't I? I bit the bullet and did the damn Thing. The 'Being a Business Celebrity' website went live and I was under the desk quaking with fear and embarrassment. I don't pretend it's easy when you start doing your Thing. It's not. Because now there's nowhere to hide! When you stand up and do your Thing it is a little bit like going naked… showing off your bare bits in all their glory (which you might have been covering up till now). But it's just as nature intended!

Doing something different can be difficult

Of course it's not always a walk in the park to step out as the naked you, especially when you're doing something quite brilliant and causing a stir. That shouldn't stop you doing it though. And actually once that initial 'Oh my gawd, I actually said that out loud' part is over then it's easy. Too easy in fact, which can then cause another type of panic.

You panic because it's easy

If, like me, you're a hard worker then when something is easy you feel bad. It's uncomfortable because surely someone somewhere is going to find out you're being cheeky and charging them for something you can do without really working all that hard. Awful!

There's my work ethic right out the window. All those hours sweating away over revision, and doing overtime at work and giving it everything in my business, slogging away… erm, apparently no need. No need at all.

More on the easy life later…

Just a note here

I'm not saying I sit around all day with my feet up sipping pina coladas now I'm doing my Thing. I do 'work' of course (this book didn't write itself!) but shhh, don't tell anyone… I actually love this work so I do it a lot, but what I am doing is EASY.

Back to my panic

So there I was panicking that I was 'pretending' to be a Business Celebrity and now there was a website showing it off. Not to mention I literally had NO IDEA who my clients were going to be. Sure, I kept meeting 'those' people at events (the ones with the neon signs above their heads saying 'not telling anyone about my Thing'), but would they 'get it' now I was 'out'. (And more importantly, would they pay for my help?)

Panic over

Turns out that when I turned up, so did my clients. And I've seen this happen a lot (like every time). Just because you can't see them yet doesn't mean they don't exist (your future clients I am talking about). In fact, more often than not it's people you already know! It very often turns out that the people you already know, who have never bought from you, suddenly turn into customers when they know your Thing. Huh, fancy that! So while you may be scratching your head thinking 'hang on a minute, I'm the same person I was yesterday', what happens is this: when you do your Thing and tell everyone what it is, people will see you in a totally different light. Imagine that… your clients were hiding in plain sight (a bit like your Thing).

You know those James Bond 'X-ray' glasses that let you really see what everyone's packing? It's pretty much like that (without the guns). You can see people's Things everywhere and they can see yours. The Things that were there all along… It's you, but you doing your Thing and people want it. That's the difference. It's totally different from you when you were just doing something you were good at…

So here I am now, finding Things and getting people famous for them. Turns out that is MY Thing. But I'm oversimplifying a little…

It wasn't that clear to start with

When I first started doing my Thing it wasn't 100% my Thing, more like 80%. Because I'd never been paid to do anything other than marketing (excluding a few random jobs such as chef, admin temp, waitress and paper girl), it never occurred to me that my Thing would be anything other than getting paid for marketing. My first strapline for Being a Business Celebrity, as I said, was 'Find out what it takes to get noticed in your market' – so, all about marketing. In fact, what I actually did was 'nail Things' too. My lovely clients kept telling me that I'd 'nailed it', I'd found the thing they did differently and more words to that effect. That was actually my Thing, but I only found out when it was pointed out to me… you could say it was on the end of my nose. Eventually I got it. I found Things. And that was the BIG Thing.

Of course...

Of course I found Things. How on earth was I supposed to do any decent marketing otherwise? There's no way you can market people and their business to stand out and get famous if you don't know what their Thing is. Obvious. Er, maybe so obvious I forgot to mention it... let alone charge for it...! Oops. And there we have it. My Thing was on the end of my own nose. Nicely pointed out to me by my own clients! I had almost worked it out by myself but I'd not seen it on its own, it was still wrapped up in something else. I was so nearly there on my own but it took the people I was doing my Thing for to really pinpoint it. Because of course, they could see it clearly.

The irony

As you can see, I had my Thing all along. It was always there. I'd always done it, I'd always seen it, I'd always known it. None of the letters after my name gave me permission to do my Thing, I gave myself permission once I'd had it pointed out to me. No-one else. I'd just made the mistake of wrapping it up in what I was good at (marketing) and not sold it on its own. The essential irony of looking for your Thing is that you have it all along. In fact, embarrassingly, you've been carrying it around slap bang in the middle of your face every single day. Everyone else can see it. It's just you that's looking straight past it. So that's why it's good to have mirrors.

Now we know what a Thing is, here's a question for you:

Are you wearing a uniform?

Much as I pretend to be super-cool (coughs), I've had to wear a number of uniforms in my life... literally in the case of school and some waitressing jobs. But even when I got to 'choose' what to wear, I still had clothes 'for work' and then 'my clothes' for the weekend. What about you? How many times have you felt like you were wearing what you were *expected* to wear versus what you actually wanted to wear? Did you feel like you were putting on a uniform?

You'll know if you're wearing one. It might be that you are literally wearing clothes that don't represent you. Or you might feel you are doing something that isn't quite 'you' – you're working in a way or in an environment that you didn't choose, it's not a perfect fit. You feel in some way that you're dressing up (or down!).

There is a perfect fit

The perfect fit is, of course, your Thing. It's when you find that 'Thing' to do that fits you just perfectly that you know you're there. You don't have to pretend any more – no more uniforms, no more putting on a show, no promoting something other than you. It's like finding the perfect dress, suit or in my case the perfect skinny jeans (legging jeans from Gap, size 26 in case you're wondering). Once you find the perfect fit you buy a pair (or two) in every colour (or maybe that's just me!).

You'll feel it more than you'll see it

Doing your Thing, finding your Thing, knowing your Thing are all very much 'feelings'-based rather than necessarily 'seeing it'. Remember, you'd be using sight when shopping at the niche supermarket and we all know how that turns out. You might 'talk yourself into' liking your niche for a while, even convincing yourself to get passionate about it but when it comes down to it, really it's just not your Thing. It's someone else's Thing that you bought into and got a bit excited about.

I've worked with people who have niched too narrowly, or just picked out a hobby they loved and tried to work it as a business thing. And while it's good to do something you love (or are good at), it's absolutely not the same as your own Thing (which is everything combined). Trust me...

Photographer for two days

Neil came to listen to a talk I was giving in London two days after taking redundancy from an investment bank. Neil is a rather good amateur photographer, and so in a 'let's do something completely different from banking' move he looked straight to his hobby and made the obvious leap to 'go pro'. Well, for two days anyway... ☺ Halfway through my talk on 'Finding your Thing' Neil realised that he wasn't actually a photographer and that his Thing was something else entirely. Something that brought together everything he'd ever done (which, in addition to banking, included being a drummer in a band!). Now the founder of International Collaboration Day, Neil has already helped engage co-working spaces in more than 30 cities globally, encouraging business relationships and serendipity in the freelance sector. Neil's Thing is now rather large, as there is a lot more still to come in the collaboration space with Neil at the helm. Neil is now only taking photos in his spare time. ☺

It might feel too small

Susannah used to be a Financial Director who was used to thinking in numbers when it came to business. But when she saw that it was the people in the business that made the extra difference she got excited about (and qualified in) coaching. When she stepped away from working in the Finance department of a business and went 'independent', she focused on coaching leaders and teams because that's where she knew the real headaches were (her business is called Aspirin by the way!). But it turns out this was too narrow a niche to allow Susannah to REALLY do her Thing. Having a strategic background meant there was so much more Susannah could add to a business than just coaching people – there's vision, strategy and knowing how to make it all sustainable. Now she's doing her Thing, bringing all her talents together in a much bigger (and more powerful) way… and curing even bigger headaches than before!

Let me tell you about jam and cake

Another way to think about the size of your Thing is to consider it in the context of afternoon tea. Often, when we find something we're really good at, we focus only on that, getting better and better at it, and making it something quite brilliant. But that thing might be jam. You may just be perfecting your recipe for jam, not realising that your Thing is a recipe for cake. Yes, your cake will taste super-yummy with your brilliant jam in between the sponges you bake, but you know how to make a cake and aren't doing that.

It's easy to forget that there is so much more sometimes in what we know and do that is relevant and can be brought to the party of our Thing than just the 'one thing' you see. My jam is marketing, I'm pretty good at it and I've spent a few years making it. But my bigger Thing is about being a Business Celebrity with all the Thing finding included too. Being a Business Celebrity is my cake.

If you just focus on the jam you miss out on sharing a bigger Thing than you think you have – however delicious that jam might be – share your sponge cake with us too! Look at what ingredients you have that add up to a cake, to make the most of your jam.

Don't expect fireworks...

Back to the dating scenario (remember that you never marry the perfect check list person – not least because I don't think they are actually real!). Personally I've never once experienced fireworks shooting out across the sky, 24 white doves being released into the air and a string quartet playing in the background at the moment of meeting someone. Instead, in my experience, it just 'felt right'. And often that moment when it 'feels right' is somewhere not very romantic either (for me it was usually a pub!) but you know when you've found the right person as everything is just 'easy'. It makes sense, it flows and it's a perfect fit. It just IS. There is no hard work or trying to force a fit. And that's exactly what finding your Thing is like. It's true love!

Expect ease

Expect me to use the word 'easy' a lot when talking about Things. Because your Thing IS easy. It's what's easy for you. It feels easy for you. It's you AT ease. All those feelings of fulfilment and satisfaction that you've been looking for – that's what is going to happen when you do your Thing. You'll feel content. So no, it's not fireworks, but they are short lived (and noisy too); instead, it's something you want to enjoy every day that's not stressful. It's not about the destination, it's about the journey – it's about doing your Thing, all the time, easily.

It's not hard work

To be an expert it's documented that you need to have done 10,000 hours of 'work'. You need to have done your Thing enough to be an expert in it, which is quite a worry if you don't know what your Thing is and you think these 10,000 hours are there stretching out in front of you like an assignment you'll need to complete before you can start with your Thing. You may think that once you find your Thing then you'll need to work hard at perfecting it and getting it just right so you can get famous for it and go out into the world and do it (and hopefully get paid for it too). You won't.

You've done your time

The good news is that you've already done your time. The hard work has happened already. You've had your Thing all along remember – it's the way that you do things, it's how you think, it's what you see and it's your take on things. Therefore, ergo, good news: you've done your time, you have your 10,000 hours of Thing-ing in the bag.

Yes of course, now you're super-clear on your Thing do go ahead and perfect it, study it more, refine it, hone it, polish it (I know I do) but you're probably now building on those 10,000 hours and working your way towards 20,000 to infinity and beyond NOT starting at 0.

You're already there

At the risk of repeating myself, here's the thing:

You already have your Thing

It's yours. You've been walking around with it all this time. On the end of your nose, remember – all you need to do now is SEE it and FEEL it. No need to go shopping for it. This isn't a quest for the holy grail – it's the age-old story of 'what you seek you already have'.

Read *The Alchemist* (if you haven't already) for a perfect illustration of that parable.

Look at you. You're already brilliant.

Why find your Thing?

Why not? It will give you a perfect outfit to wear (that doesn't feel like a uniform), the perfect work to do and a business that is easy. I'd say those are three very good reasons for starters.

Chapter 2
HOW TO FIND YOUR THING

There are only two ways to find your Thing.

Way 1: What's EASY?

Way 2: What ANNOYS you?

The end (just kidding).

I've mentioned both of them already when I talked you through me finding my Thing. And I probably laboured the 'easy' point rather a lot when I talked about uniforms. But it really is that simple, although it's not always simple to see it. Let me help…

Thing finding way 1: what's EASY?

When it comes to what you find easy, of course you can do this by yourself. Sit yourself down with a cup of tea and a blank sheet of paper and list out the things that you can do easily. And that will be a good start. But now think about this:

What are you in demand for?

Now don't think about this just in the context of 'work', think about it in the context of your whole life. Who and what are you 'the' person for.

Are you the...

- organiser
- explainer
- pacifier
- tidier
- cheerleader
- inspirer
- writer
- speaker
- leader
- teacher
- decision maker
- evaluator?

Can you...

- make the complicated simple
- pitch the right tone for everything
- find the deals
- talk to anyone

- see the wood for the trees
- juggle stuff (not literally, although maybe!)
- prioritise perfectly
- profile people
- streamline stuff
- elaborate the details
- do what needs to be done?

And the lists go on... There is some-thing that you are sought after for already. It might be your infinite wisdom and education or it might just be your energy. But start to ask what it is. And don't just think of this in 'work' terms either.

Ask and it is given

True story. If you ask the people around you – clients, friends, family (although not always as reliable that last one due to emotional bias), associates and acquaintances – to tell you what it is that they come to you for, you'll start to see what brilliant thing you are sought after for.

You won't always see it

Which is why asking other people to point it out is really important. If you can get someone who is good at Thing spotting to ask you the right questions (I might know someone... ahem) or just someone who will give you an honest answer then you start to see what's really there. Make sure who you are asking can be objective, direct and straight talking with you. And that they can challenge you too. This is not an exercise in flattery – it's an honest exercise to see what it is that you've got of value.

This is why you get a mirror (or a mentor)

Jennifer just didn't see it, but it was obvious when I looked. I don't know if you're a prolific author, but I'm not. Yes this is my second book, which means I've done it before, but it certainly doesn't take me five minutes. And I would most definitely balk at the idea of writing a novel. Even though I have probably read thousands of novels (I am that person with a double-stacked wall of bookshelves!), I would be totally stuck with where to start on writing a made-up story. And I call myself a writer.

But Jennifer wrote six novels in a year. IN A YEAR… while she was running a home staging business full time too. Oh, and being a mum to two teenagers. Hats off and hold up.

'That sounds like it must have been easy for you then?' I asked.

'Well, yes' she said, 'It was'.

'Erm…' I replied. 'So do you think everyone finds writing books quite so easy?'

'I hadn't really thought about it' was the gist of the reply…

'O…K…' (raises eyebrows) in reply. 'Yeah' (that's a face-palm moment from me). 'Hmm' I said, stating the obvious, 'maybe because you find writing so easy you might be able to help other people with their books?'

I'm paraphrasing our conversation here but you get the idea. It was just something SO easy that Jennifer didn't 'get' that other people might want this Thing. With some more exploration and more face-palming (turns out Jennifer is also a professional interviewer and someone who can just 'get' the best information out of anyone about their Thing), The Flow Writer appeared.

Now, considering Jennifer started her working life as a software engineer and her last full-time business was home staging, the writing Thing seems a departure. And yet she'd always organised thoughts and ideas, creating environments that work well... her aim was always to help other people show off their Thing in its best light (ideas, homes, work). Funny that. But actually it's not. Because as The Flow Writer, the Thing that Jennifer does best is create space that the words fill up. And then she flows that into writing, which is easy for her and not for the rest of us (and yes, she's had a hand in this book – of course – that first draft had to get out of my head somehow! Not to mention those never-ending edits...).

It might surprise you

If you've always been paid to do one thing (that you're good at) but it turns out that what people REALLY seek you out for is something else, this can be a surprise (and annoying sometimes). But do take notice. Because while you might still do your 'good at' thing at work, there will be your Thing thing too. Your Thing thing might well be something you already do as part of your work, and that's what you need to look closely at – is it the way you do something, or just a slice of your work that people always come to you for? It's not always everything that is your Thing.

So while I am 'good at' marketing, the Thing slice is Thing finding and promoting that. With Jennifer the Thing part is getting the brilliant words out of someone's head, not just 'writing a book'.

You could be really close

Your Thing might be something really really close – I am talking millimetres – to what you do already. It might be just one tiny step away, a hair's breadth, from what you 'do' right now. It's so close you can almost smell it!

But it can still feel a million miles away

If you're not there, you're not there. And actually it can be more annoying if you're super-close and STILL not there. So think like a spiral.

Curl in on your Thing

If you start working towards your Thing – getting closer and closer all the time – like you're on a spiral and working towards the centre, then you'll get there. And you'll be close enough on the way that people will help point you inwards and inwards some more. This is what happened to me. I started on the spiral of being a Business Celebrity by starting on the marketing part, but it was only when it was pointed out to me (by clients!) that Thing finding was the valuable and different part of this that I saw my Thing thing.

Or look the other way

That said. It might be that your Thing is miles away from what you 'do' right now. It could be a hobby you have, or something you do when you're 'off duty'. I've worked with people whose Thing is what they've done outside of work for 10 years or more...

Take Ben as an example. A videographer (and a good one too) by 'trade', his Thing is eating well, living well and everything it takes to 'Come Alive' (which is now the name of his business). And he's been on a personal mission to find the right foods, the right exercise, the right way to breathe even for over 10 years. I have no doubt he's done his 10,000 hours. And yet he'd never considered that as a business opportunity – after all, he's not a qualified nutritionist/personal trainer/breather, etc. Now I don't know about you, but I know I'd be happier to learn from someone who has been researching and living this for 10+ years versus someone who just got back from a 6-week course waving a certificate that says they are now 'qualified'.

Have a think about what you do when you're not 'at work' and it might just be your Thing. Drinking wine doesn't count by the way – unless you are so obsessed you tour vineyards, read everything you can on wine production and have a large cellar yourself – in which case it might well be your Thing!

It might only be a slice...

Irrespective of whether you are right next to it, or it's way over there, your Thing might also not be as big as you think it is. It might be just a slice, possibly even a sliver of what you do right now. It may be that you got so busy doing everything 'around' your Thing that it's now hard to see or even realise that your Thing is in there somewhere...

Hello?

Is anyTHING there?

I had a piece offering

My Thing is just a slice of what I used to 'do'. I've always done marketing. And I mean done it all – every part of it I could – because I thought that was the point. If I was a Marketer then I did marketing – every flavour of it I could think of. I was a marketing one-stop-shop wonder woman except, of course, that's unrealistic and very Jack-of-all-trades-master-of-none (or Jill, depending on your gender). What I am in fact brilliant at – and no sense of ego here, just what I know to be true – is seeing 'Things' in people and turning those into business and marketing strategies that make brilliant sense and fit them perfectly. That is all. I don't 'do' any marketing (apart from my own, of course, and even then it's pretty Thing related). I don't write up marketing plans – I want to cry at the thought of a giant spreadsheet marketing budget – I'm all about ideas and strategy. Put it another way – I'm a big-picture thinker, not an executor of tiny details. I don't write copy from scratch for clients (although I have been known to get my red editing pen out on occasion); I don't design brochures, plan events, manage staff, make calls for clients or attend meeting after meeting with agencies and advertisers. I used to, of course, but not any more. That's not my Thing. My Thing is just to work out which of those actions are going to get someone in their spotlight and help them brief those other people who will do the rest.

A 'not my Thing' list is a good place to start. And you just had an insight into mine… A 'not my Thing' list includes all the things I find hard (and boring – I definitely don't want to do anything that's boring!). It's the 'grind' stuff, the 'grunt work'. It's the laborious stuff. The dull stuff.

The stuff I WANT to do is all the juicy stuff. I talk a lot. I don't write it down a lot. I certainly hardly ever file and compile… details are most definitely NOT my Thing! And I used to worry about this – that I was being really lazy and selfish – but actually I'm doing my clients a disservice if I do anything that's not my Thing, as it will most certainly be someone else's. Think about that for a minute, it's a whole other way to look at your Thing and its value. Only offer what you're brilliant at.

When are you smiling?

This is a little 'life coach' territory but I have to be honest and say that finding your Thing is about your whole life. So let's look at when you're enjoying yourself. When are you grinning ear to ear? Or even just smirking a little? What's going on – literally – when you're in a good mood. When and where are you when you realise you're in flow? Where are you and what are you doing when life is good and everything just works? When are you smiling?

I know I LOVE IT when I'm with people who want to do their Thing. When I'm with one person, or a group of people who are just 'there' and ready to see it, do it, be bold with it I am very happy. A bit manic too usually (I get a lot of ideas very quickly – in fact, I've been told more than once that I think like lightening!) but that's me. Don't ever ask me to speak more slowly as I am probably already trying to. I am the Duracell bunny and I'm powered by people and their Things.

What powers you? What makes you smile? Have a think about it and write it down. Make some notes. And yes, this is an actual exercise I get people to do. The 'smile list'. It works.

Take your time

You might want to work on your 'smile list' over a few days or weeks. It's not something I would expect you to complete in 2 minutes, although if it's been brewing a while it might be that quick. Keep coming back to it. There's no rush… See what comes up. See what you notice. It's funny like that – when you start to focus on something you see it everywhere. You might start to notice much more clearly when you're smiling and when you're not. You might start to see what's there right in front of you that you love to do and what you'd rather not be doing.

And if that annoys you… then we'll move right on. As now we can look at the second way you can find your Thing.

Thing finding way 2: what ANNOYS you?

Is there something that drives you crazy? Is there something that annoys you more than other things? Maybe it's something you see every day, or maybe it's only every so often, but when you see it, you need to be held back. It's just so compelling that you want to, in fact you really need to, butt in. Like a goat… with horns. You want to CHARGE IN and say **No!!!!!!!!!!!!!!!** Because you know there is a better way, an easier way, a quicker way, a smarter way, a simpler way, a smoother way, a more purposeful way, a more contented way, a happier way, a livelier way, a something-other-than-this way. And it's really hard not to tell people. You may even interrupt them to share your way. I know I do!

And part of you also doesn't get it. I mean, it's so obvious isn't it. It's so obvious to you what this 'other way' is that you are stood there stumped – scratching your head at what seems so in-your-face obvious that not seeing it is, frankly, absurd. Like me being exasperated that people weren't profiting from their personality and putting more of themselves into their business… it's those neon signs again.

IT

WAS

SO

OBVIOUS

It was annoying… really annoying.

Here's how the annoying works

Theo doesn't get that other people find it hard to be filmed – that it's not easy to make videos about their Thing while looking relaxed and making sense on camera. He gets annoyed when he sees smart coaches and consultants and business owners not reaching/teaching all the people they could, just because they 'can't do video' or 'won't do video'.

Now I'm a little bit with Theo here (I mean, it's just talking, right?) but only because I've stared down the barrel of a video camera a lot and am quite used to it. It's odd, yes, talking to 'no-one' but I get it, and have sort of mastered it (well, I'm not scared of it which is 80% there as far as I'm concerned!). But it annoys Theo… a lot. Theo 100% gets being filmed. He worked in TV for years (not just a show either – he ran an entire channel!). He's done his 10,000 hours (and more) in front of the camera, so it's pretty easy for him…

So, we looked into this annoyance… and realised that instead of getting cross with brilliant experts not sharing their Thing on film, Theo could help them do something about it. Also turns out he had a rather clever way to do that too that didn't involve forcing anyone to stare down a camera and sweat it out. We called it 'Inclusive Video'. It's so simple, and that's also what's made it successful. With Theo as the 'linker' you don't talk to the camera about your expert Thing, you talk to Theo. Meanwhile, with all the smart things he knows, you're actually recording all your good stuff direct to camera but feel like you're just having a conversation. From annoyed to finding the answer in one simple Thing.

So, what annoys you?

What really gets your goat about…

- your industry
- your skills
- your competitors
- your market
- the marketing you see
- the ideas that aren't being shared
- the people not doing their Thing (hang on, that's mine!)
- the way something 'has' to be done
- the 'official' guide
- the legislation
- the handbooks
- the charging too much
- the charging too little
- the not seeing you can skip some steps
- the making things harder than they need to be
- people
- places
- processes

- pictures
- personalities
- posers
- procrastinators
- persecutors
- perceived wisdom
- the 'right' way?

I don't believe that *nothing* annoys you. Unless you've reached that stage of enlightenment where the world and everything in it is just Zen. In which case, Namaste. ☺ I'll wager there are more than a few things that annoy you. And even if they are annoying, they can come from a place of love.

Be annoyed with love

You need to CARE about the things that annoy you. If you don't care enough then you won't do anything. That's what being annoyed in a loving way is all about – and it's a great route to your Thing. So, when you make your list of things that annoy you, really get a feel for which of them drives you properly crazy. I mean round the bend crazy, so that you are compelled to turn it into a cause you will fight for.

> **When you get so annoyed you want to start a mission, that's the Thing**

You need to be stirred (not shaken!) to do your Thing. There needs to be something in it that means something to you. Remember I said there were two types of business owners? Those who didn't want a job and those who *had* to do their work as it was their art.

THAT'S WHAT I'M TALKING ABOUT. The art is the Thing. This Thing is your passion, it's your art, it's what you are here to do. And if someone is NOT doing it right you know you can help them do it better. And that drives you really to that point of wanting (and probably actually) butting in. You must be in that place where you want to leap out of your seat to do it. REALLY JUMP UP.

If you're not going to jump, then don't expect anyone to jump at the chance of working with you. It's only fair to be level with your expectations.

There has to be fire

When people talk about having fire in your belly, this is what I'm referring to. You need to have passion. And the passion can come from annoyance (trust me).

Passion is profitable

I know it's really hard to 'find your passion' and in fact, if you hear one more bloody person tell you they are 'really passionate' about what they do you may have to punch them (metaphorically of course!). And I totally get that. There was nothing more annoying when I was looking for my Thing and going through the grumpy phase of not knowing what it was than constantly being told to 'follow your passion' and 'do what you are passionate about' when that person may as well have been saying 'go and do the thing that you don't know what it is thing' – yeah helpful. NOT!

Your passion can be your irk

When you 'get' what annoys you (and even if you have a big list there will be a thread that links them, I promise you) then you'll start to get a feel for what drives you and what you are actually passionate about. Love and hate are most definitely two sides of the same coin and all you need to do is flip it over and work from the love.

Love is all you need

Ha, I know I've lost you now if you're not a woo woo person. That said, I was never a woo woo person either until I started to see how it all worked and what brought everything together. All you need to think about is energy, which is simple physics. We can go all science here if that's better for you than woo woo. If you do your Thing from a place of ANGER and pure annoyance, your energy will be aggressive. But if you do your Thing from a place of annoyance where you can bring LOVE (i.e., solve the problem and make the world a better place), you'll have a really attractive and strong energy.

Think of anyone who has tried to 'recruit' you into something that they are passionately aggressive about – whether that's joining them at 'their' gym, getting involved in a multi-level marketing business, or even just buying into the RIGHT way to do something. It's scary. You immediately want to step back. It's the energy of a desperate salesperson (think last-day-of-the-month commission hungry here!). It's not nice to be on the receiving end of that energy, ever.

I don't have a fancy equation

Bearing in mind my BSc is in Social Sciences (Economics and Politics, if you remember) and not a 'white coat' science, I am not going to give you an equation for this, but I'm sure you can get 'the vibe'. No-one is going to want your Thing if it's angry and aggressive but if it's in an energy of ease, enjoyment and improvement then bingo you're in.

What annoys you is an answer

People will pay for answers. If someone has a question or a problem that needs solving, they are looking for an answer. When what annoys you is a problem you have the answer to, then that's a valuable Thing. What you now need to do is shape it up into a process or philosophy that people can easily understand and use. That's how you'll make money from your Thing.

You only have one Thing!

This is something I get asked ALL the time. 'Can I have more than one Thing?' To which the answer is, NO. Now that is not to say you don't have a number of ways in which you DO your Thing, but they are expressions or flavours of your Thing, not different Things. There is something you are uniquely brilliant at – and you may arrive at that result 10, 100 or 1000 ways but this is your gift, your brilliant Thing. This is when you're totally in your flow and doing your best work.

Think of your Thing as the boss

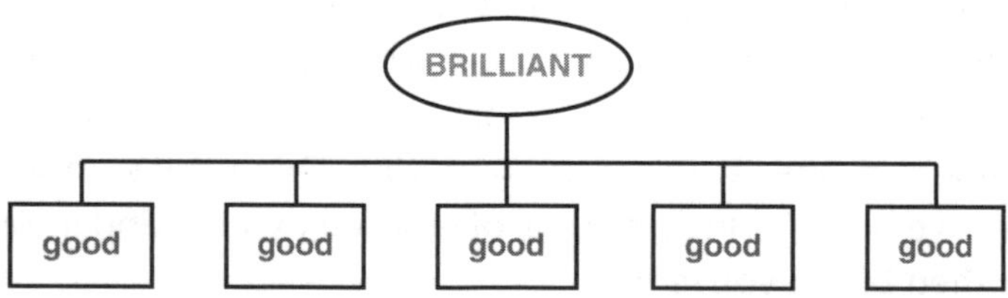

Your Thing is in charge

My business is called 'Being a Business Celebrity', but in essence, what I am always doing when I do my Thing is giving people CLARITY. The five steps of my process (see below) are the departments in my organisation and the boss of everything is CLARITY. It doesn't matter which department I am working in – whichever way I am doing or expressing my Thing – I am always working with the intention to provide clarity. It's always about helping someone get clear. That's my intention with VIP clients, people who watch my free classes, even lovely people like you who read my book. My absolute boss-of-everything aim is that you get clear. Or at least clearer.

To understand your Thing better, have a look and see where the different parts of it fit. Work out which are departments and ways of doing your Thing, and what is the ultimate result. Always ask 'what does this really do?' when you find a piece of your Thing.

Here's how my Thing looks:

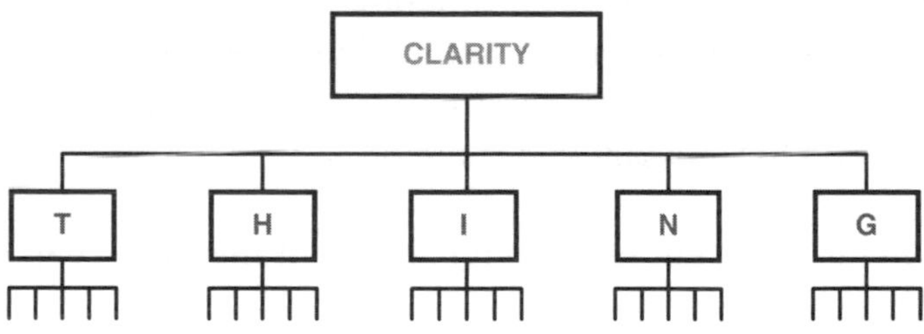

I'll be talking about philosophies in the next chapter (as this is how you explain and easily sell your Thing), but you might get the idea when I say that my five 'departments' are also my philosophy –

my five steps to being a Business Celebrity:

1. Find Your **T**hing
2. **H**ave a Fame Name®
3. **I**nteresting Stories Sell
4. **N**othing is Impossible
5. **G**et in Your Spotlight

Now of course these departments also have sub-departments, just like a real business organisation chart – where the sales department, for example, will have online, offline, direct, customer services, channel sales and all sorts. For me, 'Get in Your Spotlight' (my step 5) is a long (long!) list of marketing 'how to' and ideas. But I've grouped them all under that heading to make it simpler for people to understand. Each main department is one of the ways you do your Thing. And in charge of it all – the boss – is your Thing. For me, that is CLARITY.

Be the boss

When you're looking for your Thing and asking yourself 'is this it, or is this it?' start to build an organisation chart around these answers. See what the end result of doing everything is. Keep going 'up' the organisation chart and see where it goes. You are always trying to work out who is the boss.

Here are the questions you should ask about the things you do:

- What does that give?
- What's the *real* result of that?

Then you can get to see more clearly what's a department, a sub-department, or the ultimate Thing 'above' those. It doesn't matter what stage or part of the 'Being a Business Celebrity' process I am working through with someone – the ultimate outcome I always want is clarity. Clarity on their Thing, clarity on their Fame Name® and message, getting clear on their story, clearly knowing it's possible and being clear on a marketing and spotlight plan. Clarity, however it's needed. And that's how I got to my departments and the Thing that sits above all of them. I asked the questions.

The hierarchy is important, as otherwise you might get stuck thinking your Thing is smaller than it really is (as you pick a department or sub-department and label that your Thing). Keep on thinking bigger and see where your things ultimately lead you to your BIG Thing.

Easy or annoying – ask the questions

Whether you found your Thing through looking at what you find easy or you found your Thing through what annoys you, you need to get to the TOP of it. You must see what the boss is, otherwise you'll get stuck.

Stuck in a department

We're back in the niche supermarket now, picking something off the shelf again. If you pick one of your departments (or worse still, one of your sub-departments) as your niche – or Thing – then you'll get stuck. You'll feel (like I did when I 'picked' travel and hotel marketing) that you've niched yourself into a corner. It's not big enough for you to express yourself fully and you'll feel frustrated that your talents are constrained or are being overlooked. Now I love all my departments and I love all the ways that I 'do' my Thing but I can tell you right now, if I ONLY did one of them and did it over and over I'd be bored. Doing just one department or 'way' of my Thing over and over would be super-dull. But that's what happens when you pick a department as a niche or label it your Thing. That's why it's important to think BIG with your Thing, not niche it down small. When you don't give yourself enough room to play you'll get bored (and frustrated!) pretty quickly. There's time to think about niching later – right now we want to see how BROAD this Thing can be.

Only one person gets to hang out in every department

And that person is the boss, which is why your Thing is the boss – it's the ultimate overseer and 'in charge' of you doing all the different parts of your Thing. You can of course choose to hang out in one department for a while, a long while if you want to, but your Thing remains your Thing.

Let's get Jamie Oliver to explain

Not only does Jamie have a great Fame Name® – The Naked Chef (more on those in Chapter 4) – he is also a great example of having individual projects as departments without getting stuck in them as his only niche (or mistaking them for his overall Thing). Jamie started out as The Naked Chef. No, not cooking without clothes on ☺ but instead bringing us back to basics, naked 'pukka' food with simple, fresh ingredients. And yes, I remember when it was just him on his scooter zipping to the market and sliding down the banisters of his London pad. And Jamie still *is* The Naked Chef, but he's had several different projects.

Projects as departments

Projects can be niches that you want to hang out in but not choose as your only Thing for ever, and this is a good way to do your Thing if you want to have more than one 'specialism' or 'market'. You do projects – while your Thing (the overall boss) remains the same.

Here's how Jamie did it

Jamie has always been (and will always be) The Naked Chef. Even if he has stopped using the name, he'll always be a chef whose values are good, fresh, honest, 'naked' food. While he started out just 'teaching us to cook', he then went on to do his Thing as different projects. We've seen Jamie do:

- school dinners
- ditching the junk food (when he went to the USA)
- Italian
- how to cook
- Fifteen Foundation (helping young people)
- 30-minute meals
- 15-minute meals
- great British food
- low-cost meals

not to mention opening quite a few restaurants along the way (my favourite being Fifteen Cornwall hanging off a cliff over a surf beach) and generally showing up on TV a lot. ☺

But all the time he was doing his Thing

So you can choose a niche project, without worrying about getting stuck in it for ever, because whatever project you're working on and whatever way you're doing it, you're still doing your Thing. And your Thing is the boss. Your Thing never stops being the boss.

Chapter 3

DOING YOUR THING

Now, it's one thing to find your Thing and another to do something with it. After all, there's no point sitting at home on your own being amazing. Nothing is going to happen that way. And you're certainly not going to help anyone. Your Thing is an answer. It's a solution to someone else's problem. So go use it to fix things!

Here's what you can do with your Thing:

- You can do your Thing for someone – after all, you find it easy and they don't.
- You can teach your Thing to someone – so you can pass on your 'easy' way.
- You can teach your Thing to someone so they can do it for someone else – you can even build up a team of people who 'Thing' like you do so you don't have to do it all.

- You can record you doing your Thing and share it that way (so you only have to 'do' it once).
- You can show someone the steps to your Thing so they can see how it works and go do it themselves.
- You can write about your Thing and share it in words so you can tell a lot of people about it at once.
- You can do your Thing for individuals, groups, companies, governments, the entire planet. How big you do your Thing is up to you.

But if you don't do it, no-one gets the answer that you have and we all stay where we are.

Make your Thing easy to follow

Now there's a little hurdle here, in that because you do your Thing automatically – that's why it's so easy for you – you don't always see how it works. Your Thing is what's called your 'unconscious competence' (one of the four stages of competence in Psychology). It is what you might describe as 'second nature' to you, or as I call it 'common sense'.

Your common sense is yours

Aside from the obvious pieces of common sense – 'don't touch fire' and 'don't eat yellow snow', etc. there will also be YOUR common sense. This will be your Thing. There will be all those 'obvious' pieces of understanding and insight that you have where you assume (big assumption by the way) that everyone else has this 'common sense' too. Wrong! There is a chunk of common sense that you have but other people don't. It's the common sense you worked out through your experience and learning and take on things. And that is why you get annoyed when you see what you consider to be 'common sense' not happening. If the other people knew what you knew they'd be doing it!

Take on me

This is a real 'A-ha' moment (sorry, 1980s pop joke there). You already have your Thing, it's your list of common sense rules and it's how you see the world. Your Thing is your take on things.

Now you see it, now you don't (know what to do with it)

The challenge you have now with your Thing (and where my Thing comes into its own) is sharing your Thing with everyone who needs it. This is where you might need some help in doing your Thing. And you might need to bend your head a little to see how your Thing can be of value, as you may think you can't sell common sense. You may feel that's a bit 'Emperor's new clothes'... Wrong. Everyone needs common sense. You can never have too much.

I am sure you can...

- save people money
- do something faster they want done faster
- make something bigger they want bigger (no sniggering at that one)
- make something smaller they want smaller

- save people time
- save people thinking
- be smarter
- be more inventive
- be more efficient
- be more exciting
- make people feel happy
- make people calm
- give confidence
- give clarity (that's my one)
- give peace of mind
- give direction

and the list goes on… These are all 'Thing' outcomes; your Thing will do one or more of these. And here's the thing – ALL of these Things are VALUABLE – maybe not to everyone, but there are enough people who will pay you for them. Some people are happy doing DIY and taking things the slow way. But some people want the answer, they want the fix and they want it NOW. And they will pay NOW. And that's how you turn your Thing into a business.

Find the way they want to pay for

This is how you make money from your Thing. This is how you help people with your Thing.

Don't give it all away for free!

If you remember nothing else from reading this book, remember:

Your Thing is valuable

Repeat after me:

MY THING IS VALUABLE.

JUST BECAUSE I FIND IT EASY DOESN'T MEAN I DON'T CHARGE FOR IT.

MY EASY IS NOT YOUR EASY.

I HAVE THE ANSWER YOU WANT, AND I'D LIKE YOU TO PAY FOR IT PLEASE.

THANK YOU.

Of course you can still help for nothing. I'm a big fan of tasters. In fact, you can always give away a lot of information but when it comes to action – make sure that's paid for. ☺

Note on free

It's important to know (and I've tested this enough!) that typically when you give away your Thing for free, it's never valued as highly as when it's paid for. I know that when I've paid for help I'll do what I'm told or the job gets done right away (and properly!). If you give it all away, no-one is going to get anywhere near the results they will if you charge for it. So, you really must see the VALUE in your Thing and make sure it's paid for. Because, actually, then it will give the results you know it can.

You need a plan, Stan

So that you can easily convey the value of your Thing, you need a simple way of explaining your Thing to other people so they 'get' it; they get how you do it and they get what it can do for them. It might be a process or a blueprint or a philosophy or a set of principles – anything that is simple, straightforward to understand and sets out what you do in a clear way. You need a plan for Stan, and anyone else who needs your Thing.

Step back and take a good look

When you know what your Thing is – you've got to the root of that annoyance and answered it with your 'easy' – you need to spell out how it works. Think 'My Thing for Dummies'. Make it super-simplistic: one step at a time. No confusion, no jargon (don't get me started on that), but plain language and simple steps that show how you do what you do so we (i.e. the general public) get it.

Mine has five

To keep it simple, I recommend that you too have five steps, or elements, or pieces to your process or philosophy. You can have four or six or seven; I wouldn't go less and I wouldn't go more (starts to counteract that simplicity rule). Also, there is a line of argument that odd numbers are better. It's possibly just 'one of those things', but I always take notice of 'those things' so it might be worth thinking about and sticking with an odd number. Let's put it this way – most of the time, when I work with people to work out Thing philosophies, we aim for five parts. It's nice and tidy, provides a tipping point in the middle at step 3, and is enough steps to look smart but not so many as to confuse. So for now, go with five.

Here are mine as a reminder:

1. Time to Find Your **T**hing
2. **H**ave a Fame Name®
3. **I**nteresting Stories Sell
4. **N**othing is Impossible
5. **G**et in Your Spotlight

These are the five steps to 'Being a Business Celebrity' – this is my process. It shows the progression of stages you go through when you work out your Business Celebrity business.

Obviously, step 1 is that you have to find your Thing. You pretty much can't do anything without that (skip back to Chapter 2 now if you need to look through that again).

Then you work out a Fame Name® at step 2 so you can tell everyone else what it is that you do that's brilliant AND it helps you own it too (more on that in Chapter 4).

Interesting stories are the easiest way to market yourself as they sell for you. Chapter 5 takes you through the story-telling know how.

Nothing is impossible is a step I didn't realise was needed at first, until it struck me that it's the most important step in the entire process. D'oh! If you don't believe in your Thing then no-one else is going to either (which will show up as no sales). Chapter 6 dives into that in more detail.

Get in your spotlight at step 5 is where I finally get to the marketing piece – the only piece I used to 'sell' and the only thing I thought I could get paid for... See how much bigger my Thing is than I first thought? Watch out for that last step.

For me, the last step was the only one I had ever been paid for before and I used to wrap every other step that came before it up in 'free consultation' or 'part of the process'. And this is when you can start to look samey. I had made the assumption that 'everyone' did what I did before they did the marketing piece at the end. I was wrong. I was bundling everything together so that my Thing was disguised (to the point of almost total camouflage!) and it just 'looked like' marketing from the outside. Think about that – now I have 80% more that I talk about (the first four steps) than the last 20% (step 5 – the marketing part), which was all I ever used to mention!

> **While I was desperately trying to stand out I was disguising my difference**

I see that ALL the time. You don't 'see' the different steps you have in what you do. You wrap it all up in 'everyone does that' assumptions or 'but that's just common sense' excuses. Big mistake. HUGE.

> **You don't see what you have**

So while you may see your BIG Thing as an outcome, you might not see its components and moving parts. But those are what sells it and sets you apart.

You have to look under the bonnet

Your Thing has an engine. Now as someone who has NO CLUE about how any type of engine actually works, I can 100% sympathise if you can't see the engine of your Thing right now. Surely you just put petrol in and it goes, right? Anything else, call the RAC... ☺ But you should get to know your own engine. Work out what pistons fire what cylinders and make stuff go… er, might have mechanically lost myself in my own metaphor here but you get the idea.

You need to know how it works… because this is how you sell your Thing

When you can explain step by step how your Thing works – the pieces or steps it is made up from – you have a clear plan for delivery. This is *super-important* if you are selling a service. It's also important if you have a product too, but that's easier to spell out – that's about pre-sales qualifying, finding the right fit, delivering the product, checking it's working as sold, providing maintenance (as a simple example).

When you have a service, what makes it easier to sell – or better, easier to buy – is that there's an end. You're selling something finite. In reality, there are often loops and re-runs but to start out with, having an end point is highly reassuring to a buyer of your Thing as a service.

Have an end

Buying something that could go on and on and on is hard to say yes to. I don't know about you, but there's no way I would sign up to personal training, or French lessons 'for ever'. But I'd certainly be interested in 'Get fit for your holiday in 6 weeks' or 'Have a conversation in French in 10 lessons', etc. There is an end. Now I also realise that I could in fact have a personal trainer for ever as being fit for ever is a very good idea, but it would freak me out to 'buy' that at the beginning. The same goes for French lessons. Obviously, like most languages, you could carry on learning for life (let's be honest, I'm not even sure I've fully mastered English yet and I've had a few decades!).

What would be even better is if the personal trainer or French teacher told me the exact steps they were going to take me through and where what I was buying ended (or where I could take a break). It might be the 6-week fitness programme or 10 lessons of French covered all of their steps and philosophy – just in a limited way. Or I might know I am only buying steps 1 and 2 and to get the rest will take longer, for example. It doesn't matter to me, I just know there's an end and what I am getting doesn't carry on for ever. It's too scary to commit to for ever in most instances!

Your end doesn't have to be your everything

When I work with people to package their Thing for sale, I map out their products and services on a 'Star Plan'. A 'Star Plan' has five points of entry (or levels of service) covering free through to VIP, and we use the pieces of their philosophy or process to build up the different packages. It may be that every product and service has every step included (with a start and a finish point). It may be instead that some products and services are just one or two of the steps, in which case it's clear what you DO get and what you DON'T get… and that there is an end.

> **No-one wants to buy forever, they want to buy an answer for now**

Remember, you are selling an answer. Your Thing is an answer to a problem that people have. Not all people need your Thing (never make that mistake) – but some people do. And those people REALLY need your help. They REALLY need your Thing. But if you can't explain your Thing clearly, and show them the steps and pieces of how it works, you make it hard for them to buy. If it's one big lump of a Thing it's not easy to see how it works. It looks too big, too intangible, too much, too lumpy.

Big fluffy clouds

When you find your Thing, if you don't have a philosophy or process that clearly explains it step by step, you have a fluffy cloud Thing. It's very pretty and contained but it's not clearly defined – not to mention it can change shape as the wind blows! When you first find your Thing it will often look like a cloud. Your next job is to shape it and put it into a box.

You need to box it up

As a 'creative entrepreneur type' it pains me to say this, but you do need to put yourself in a box. When your Thing is in a box you can clearly label it and put it up for sale. Then, when people like the look of the label, they'll read the ingredients and see what's included (those are your steps).

Like picking up a book…

This book is called *Find Your Thing*. You picked it up because you 'got' the title. Then you read the blurb (probably) and it spelled out for you what's inside. You then checked out the chapters to see step by step what was going to be covered. This book is my Thing in a box. It's a really good plan to put your Thing in a box, with a list of ingredients clearly displayed if you want to sell it easily. People like to know what they are buying.

Think slices or steps

Unpack your Thing so you can see how it works. Really pull it apart and see what it is that you do when you do what you do. It might be that you have 'steps you go through before you do what you think is your Thing' (it's all your Thing). Work out 'what you stand for' and piece this together as a philosophy.

It can be a cake

If there is no natural progression to your Thing – that is, do this, then that, walking people through a process and steps – then think cake. A whole cake is made up of slices (if you're willing to share!) and you need ALL the slices to make a cake complete, but you can also serve each slice on its own. When you have a 'slices' philosophy for your Thing then you're saying 'the pieces all work on their own and are helpful but when you have them ALL then you have a complete answer'.

Let's go back to our personal trainer example and say that their philosophy for 'being fit' is made up of five factors – for example, eating, sleeping, exercising, focusing and hydrating. And they have their 'own take' on those five elements (ideally with their own language too – this helps to emphasise the uniqueness of their Thing). Now to get 'fitter', even if I just had a slice of their Thing (realising the irony of using a cake analogy with a personal trainer!) would be a result. If I just ate better or slept more or drank more water my body would be fitter.

Results

A result can be enough. You don't always have to deliver THE result. Selling a result on its own works. It can be a great start. So if you have a step-by-step Thing, or a sliced-up Thing, you can sell a piece on its own if it gives a result.

Always talk about THE result!

It's important when you talk about your Thing that you always make it super-clear what it ALL looks like, and the total philosophy or process that you have – for optimum fitness you clearly need all five factors of eating, sleeping, exercising, focusing and hydrating, for example. But you don't have to sell it all at once. You could start with the one that gives the quickest/most visible result. I'd go for sleep myself! Make it clear what's included (and what's not) in your 'a result' offer of course. But know you don't have to offer everything you have all at once.

This is a VERY IMPORTANT POINT. You can get over-excited. There is nothing wrong with over-delivering in terms of service, but it's not always a good plan to over-deliver your Thing, because your entire Thing in one go might be way too much for people to handle! And I know you're bursting to share it all now, but be nice. Don't overwhelm people (otherwise you'll create more problems than you solve!). You can be even nicer and spoon-feed people what they need as and when they need it. Phew. Relax.

You can deliver your Thing one piece at a time

If it is clear from the start that your Thing can be delivered step by step, then there's no need to force-feed people all your Thing at once! Eek. Talk about overstuffing (or overwhelming, as it will feel like to them). Because you've been smart and set out your Thing one step or one slice at a time, you're able to sell it a step or a slice at a time too. This also shows how much MORE VALUE there is in your Thing.

Each piece is gold

When you sell your Thing as an all-in-one it's hard to see the value of the different component pieces, which means it's also going to be hard to charge for each step or slice on its own. I'll be honest here, I never realised I could charge for 'Thing finding'! Instead, I had it all wrapped up so tightly as part of 'doing marketing' that there wasn't any room to charge for it. In fact, it didn't even occur to me to charge for it at all. I saw it as 'all part of the service'. But that's where you can go wrong.

Every part of your Thing is value packed

So by unpacking it and seeing it piece by piece you can add more value to your clients and your own bank balance at the same time. And yes, now I get paid just to find Things. I also get paid just to work out Fame Names, or work on stories, or get spotlight marketing done. All pieces of a bigger Thing, which I used to sell as just one Thing before I realised there was more to it.

Get philosophical

Work out the pieces of your Thing and share them as a whole. Get clear on your manifesto or your method. See what your steps are, or your system is. Work out the process or principles of your Thing.

Then cut that up too

You can slice and dice some more. There will be sub-departments of these departments of your Thing (because that's what we've been talking about). Some of these tiny slices you might sell on their own, or include, or give away. But they are important to share too. The detail is your diligence.

When you can show the top-level Thing, the philosophy or process underneath, then the tiny details that make it all up, there's no arguing that you know your stuff. You have built up your Thing credibility by showing that you have all the components and can reach the ultimate result.

Confidence sells Things

Confidence sells you and your Thing. And if you're clear, you'll be confident. To demonstrate clarity you need to be able to explain your philosophy or process. When YOU know how your Thing works (and can explain it simply, step by step) it's not going to be hard to sell it to other people as you'll be clear and confident about it. It really is as simple as that. Have you ever bought from someone who waffled on and on about what they do, and never quite explained it clearly? Didn't think so…

Why clarity matters

No-one will buy your Thing if they are not clear about what it will do for them. It's the marketers' radio station joke – what channel should you be tuned into when marketing your business? WII FM – What's In It For Me. Guffaw…

(Sorry, us seasoned marketers had to live through the days of direct mail envelope-stuffing machines and endless days of manning exhibition stands; forgive us our bad jokes – they kept us going.)

When you have a clear philosophy or process, it's super-obvious what your Thing will do for people. You can show them the journey or the complete outcome. There's no way they won't know what's in it for them as your Thing is ALL about them and how you can help. Not if you waffle though… so don't skip this part, if you do it's going to make everything else so much harder. And messy. Very messy.

Things need labels

When I said your Thing is your gift I meant it. Think of it all wrapped up in nice paper, with a gift tag on it clearly labelled with who it's for. And add the sentiment for the occasion. THEN you know it will be accepted and received by the right person. You want to give your Thing only to people who need it and WANT IT. It is very important that they want it.

Not everyone wants a gift

Odd as this may sound, you need to know that not everyone wants your Thing, even if they need it. In fact, the irony is that usually the people that need your Thing the most are the ones who ask for it the least. Hmm, one of life's little mysteries there.

Only give your Thing to people with their hands up

You want to give your Thing to people who already have their hands up for it – 'pick me, pick me' style. If you want to give yourself a big job and a huge challenge (usually unrewarding), then please go ahead and try to 'convince' people they need your Thing. Get their arm and try to force it up into the air. Keep pushing; go on, you know you can do it. Even though they are resisting, you keep sweating and pushing because you KNOW the difference it will make when you help them, and yes it would be huge. But they don't want it . . . I really encourage you not to waste time trying to convince anyone of the brilliance of your Thing. It can be the quickest route to disheartenment and defeat.

This is when it feels like sales

You know that icky feeling you get when someone is on a mission to 'sell' you something. Or that uncomfortable feeling you get when someone is pressuring you into something (we've talked about this already – when someone is aggressively passionate). Perhaps it's just simple annoyance that they are not listening to what you have to say and carrying on anyway.

I love it when we get people knocking on our door to sell 'home improvements' when clearly our entirely renovated house (with a full set of brand new windows staring out at them) is presenting itself as obvious evidence that we don't need their services. And *still* they start their spiel. ARGH. Yes that.

I Do Not Have My Hand Up!

The opposite is also true:

Don't NOT sell your Thing because you're worried there are no people with their hands up

Biggest mistake ever, that one. Just because you might not have met these people yet it doesn't mean they don't exist. When you first work out your Thing, if you're not thinking like an entrepreneur yet, your next thought will probably be 'no-one will buy that'. But how do you know? Don't be defeated before you start. You've not asked anyone yet!

I had a handful of people in my head who might be 'vaguely interested' in Being a Business Celebrity when I started (those people with neon signs I'd been meeting). And that was it. I certainly didn't have a 'list' of ready-to-buy clients. And I didn't really know exactly what this ideal client of mine looked like. I had to go and make my noise and see who paid attention. It turns out, however, there are plenty of people who hadn't found their Thing yet, or didn't know how to get famous for it, so I needn't have worried! I just spoke out (marketing in other words) to the people who did have their hands up.

Clarity is your checklist

When you are clear on your Thing, and how it works, then you can get clear on who needs it. Your clients will be super-clear if it's what they need or not, as you've clearly explained it to them! You can see who does and doesn't have their hands up because you know what you're looking for. You know what people will have their hands up for.

Watch out for misdirection

Sometimes you want to think a little laterally when it comes to what 'hands up' looks like in the market for your Thing. It has been known for people to have their hands up for the wrong thing when really they need your Thing. Here's how that works. Let's say you help people get confident. You help with stress and overwhelm/focus (or lack of it). Your boss Thing might be calm. So you're looking for people who have their hands up to the problem of 'help me, I am super-stressed' – and you will find some people saying that directly. But you might also find their hands up for what they 'think' is the answer to the problem of being super-stressed... There will be hands up for spa weekends and mindfulness retreats. There will be hands up for yoga. Look for hands up for moving to the countryside, or moving to an entirely different country. There will be hands up for finding a new job, or changing career. Misdirection in many cases; all these example hands-up situations could also be a call for calm.

So, think 'around' your Thing and work out where those hands are in the air and what for. Some will be right in front of you and some a little to the side...

Get decisions

Get this clear. You're never looking to convince anyone to buy your Thing. However, you're also not looking to leave someone undecided. You absolutely need to be detached from the outcome (so no getting stressed about those people who don't put their hands up even though they clearly need your help). You need to be okay that you can't help everyone because not everyone wants to be helped. Don't get me started on this one. I see 'Things' everywhere. Literally everywhere. And if I'm not seeing Things I'm seeing 'get famous' ideas for Things that are already there. It's like radar I can't switch off. But I have to be okay if it doesn't always resonate or isn't always wanted. It's not my job to convince. I work with the already convinced and so should you. So, all you need to remember is that your aim is always to get a decision. A 'no' is as good as a 'yes' (although you won't get paid for it!). The worst thing you can ever do for someone who is considering your Thing is to leave them undecided. Indecision is uncomfortable, so get decisions...

Serve and solve

What you need to do with your Thing is serve with it. No, not like in a game of tennis – don't go lobbing it at people! Not unless they have their hands up to catch it. ☺ Your role is to help, assist and improve – to serve by solving. Because your Thing is the answer to someone else's problem, it's your duty (yes I will get pedantic about this) to do your Thing so you can serve who you are here to serve (the people who are asking for it).

It doesn't involve bowing

You don't have to bow and scrape before people to serve them. It's not about being subservient; it's about serving them with the gift of your Thing. It's actually about sharing and not being selfish.

Actually, it's not about you

Much as I want you to find YOUR Thing, it's not actually about you. Er, did I not mention that? Apologies. But here's the thing – it's about you SHARING your Thing with the people who need it. If you have the answer to a problem and you're not sharing it, well that just makes you rather selfish I'm afraid.

Don't be selfish

If you sit at home on your own being amazing then you're not helping anyone. Your Thing isn't there to be admired – it's there to be DONE and shared. If you're doing your Thing then there is benefit being shared. There are results happening and transformations taking place. That's the whole point of this.

It's about the pebbles

I love talking about my Thing, and I love sharing the Thing-finding Thing too. But there are lots of other things I could be doing, like taking my small people out on adventures, or baking (I do love cake), or reading and learning, or swimming. I could be eating a nice meal or drinking wine. But right now this minute I am writing this for you as a pebble. When I do my Thing and help someone else find their Thing this is me throwing a pebble in the water, the ripples then spread out and before you know it there are waves everywhere. And this is exactly the same for your Thing too. It can create waves if you throw pebbles.

I have a big mission

I have a mission in life, and it's quite large. I want **everyone** doing their Thing. And I can either try and tell everyone one person at a time or I can lob a few pebbles. When my pebbles hit the right ponds (yes, metaphorically I may have just called you a pond – sorry!) then they cause ripples. And these ripples spread out, creating waves to catch more people in their wake before they reach the shore.

I'm hoping you'll make waves

When you work out your Thing, it's going to allow other people to do theirs – either directly or by default. And so if you are the pond, then this book is the pebble and I have started a lot of rippling waves that are way more movement than I can create on my own by speaking to one person at a time. And you need to make waves too. You need to work with people and businesses to solve their problems so they are in a better place now they have your Thing. This will then give them more time or energy or ideas to focus on doing their Thing too. We're all in this together.

The more people there are doing their Thing, the more productive and focused and happier everyone is going to be. If everyone is doing what they find easy, imagine the satisfaction that will abound. Not to mention if we're all solving what annoys us, then that angry energy will disappear too. I get that this is really 'big picture' stuff, but you need to think that big with your Thing too. Don't let it just be about the people you can help one at a time, see what waves can be created from that impact too.

You need to show off your Thing

This is the 'get famous' part and explains why I think that is important. If you find your Thing and then keep it to yourself no-one gets to benefit. It's like you painted the Mona Lisa and then shoved it in the attic. Art is there to be seen and admired and enjoyed. It's the same with your Thing. It's to be USED. It's to be DONE. It's there for a reason… and that reason isn't just for you to know. You need to display your Thing. You need to…

- write about it
- speak about it
- shoot video about it
- blog about it
- Facebook about it
- Tweet about it
- walk down the street with a sandwich board about it (maybe)
- get on the radio about it
- tell us on TV about it
- get interviewed about it
- broadcast it
- wear a T-shirt showing it

- get out a megaphone and shout about it (okay, maybe not that one literally either).

In short:

You need to get visible

Cue PANIC!

Yup.

Sorry.

The game's up.

This 'Find Your Thing' thing isn't going to let you go quietly.

You need to get visible.

If you want to really do your Thing you need to get visible, and show up shouting (nicely) about your Thing. We need to hear from you and learn about your Thing. We need to see and hear why it's so right for us. We know we have problems, but what we don't know yet is how you solve them. We will know how you solve our problems if you tell us though…

Time to stand up and be counted

Things are only useful when they are being done, so it's time to do yours. Your fans are waiting. Yes, they are. Really.

PART TWO

GETTING FAMOUS FOR YOUR THING

Chapter 4

FAME NAME®

This is what I am 'famous for' and ironically, while I would like to think *my* Fame Name® is 'Manager of Business Celebrities', often I am known as 'The Fame Name® Lady'. But that still works, as if you Google Fame Name® you'll find me. ☺ And that's what a Fame Name® is all about – being remembered and being found. It's your **personal headline** that gets you noticed for your Thing. It also has a rather special side-effect. It makes you OWN your Thing too…

Why now?

Having laboured the point (if you missed it, read Chapter 3 again!) that you must DO your Thing, my attitude is that you must just get on with it. Yes, you could sit at home and contemplate your navel for a while, or you could just get it together and get out there and start getting noticed. Claim your space. Do your Thing. Tell us what it is! You're going to have to get famous at some point so I'm a 'jump in at the deep end' kinda girl. If you're going to do it, do it. No point being 'a little bit' famous. Having a Fame Name® whips you out of obscurity and into a spotlight sharpish. It also makes you own your Thing and gives you confidence.

It's the fastest way I know

A Fame Name® is the fastest way I know to own your Thing and get famous for it (short of making front-page news). When you start telling people succinctly and directly what it is that you can do for them, they'll start to take notice and remember you. It's not always easy at first (deep breath time), but once you've started you'll see the effects and won't worry about it anymore. Everyone who has their hands up for your Thing will see you and what you can do for them. And that can only be a good thing if you're looking to have them buy your Thing.

Examples

Here are some famous people you might know; the rest had a little bit of help from me…

Supernanny

Queen of Shops

The Naked Chef

The Juice Master

The Galloping Gourmet

The Book Midwife

The Flow Writer

The Business Locksmith

The Why Parent

The Direction Finder

The Skin Energy Doctor

The Systems Superwoman

The Sales Sculptor

Queen of Calm

The Chief Resilience Officer

The Courage Angel

The Parenting Pacemaker

The Soothe Operator

The Social Marketing Queen

The Head Fixer

The Ideas Implementer

The Disruption Doctor

The Truth Teacher

The Tech Untangler

It makes you sticky

A Fame Name® will make you stick in people's heads. And this is a good thing, as you'll get remembered and referred to for your Thing. Referrals are one of THE best ways of marketing yourself. The conversions you'll get from a referral are likely to be the highest you'll have from any type of marketing effort, as who doesn't take a personal recommendation seriously? I can even prove this to you (digs out MBA thesis) as the research I did into what marketing activity works best at generating sales was, you guessed it, referrals (admittedly this was in the software industry, but it's pretty indicative of most markets based on my wider reading and experience). So, make sure you're sticky.

The science part!

This is why Fame Names work. There is a principle in psychology called the Baker/baker paradox, and it explains how our brains remember people. Our brains are wired to remember someone for what they DO much more than what their NAME is. So in the example given, if you meet a baker (i.e., purveyor of fine patisserie) you are much more likely to remember that than if you meet 'Mr John Baker' and you have to remember his name. It's just what we do in our heads when we meet people. Think now – can you remember some people you met at a networking event or a party and remember what they do but can't quite remember their actual name (let alone their surname?). That's the science part of Fame Names working right there.

I realised the accuracy of the Baker/baker principle when I was on holiday once, having a conversation at dinner with my husband about various people I'd chatted to that day – along the lines of 'you know so and so who used to be a chef, she's married to the investment guy, and then I was talking to the PR lady….' I couldn't remember their actual names easily but I knew exactly what they did for a living.

We don't remember names well

But we do remember what people DO. So that's what's given in a Fame Name®. We tell people our Thing so they remember us for what we do. We play into their hands and their brain waves. There's no point trying to rewire everyone's brain (a tad on the megalomaniac side), instead work with what you've got – an audience of people who will literally remember you for what you do. So give them a good name to remember.

I'll bet in your mobile phone right now you have things like 'Dentist, Doctor, Hairdresser, Taxi' and their numbers but you won't always have those people's names. Or you might be like me and have a weird hybrid name in your phone like 'Sarah-Louise Beauty' (she does my nails) and 'Nicola Hair' (not her actual surname but she's obviously my hairdresser). These are shorthand Fame Names to help my brain out. ☺

Instant identity

We'll know straight away if we need you and your Thing when we hear your Fame Name®. It's pretty clear if you're for us and your Thing will help. I'll know right away if you can solve MY problem. It's SO CLEAR that no mistakes are likely, which is why Fame Names work so well. You're being BOLD and CLEAR about who you are. It's a beacon of plain talking. Your Thing is your Thing. No quibble and no question. We're tuned in right away to that radio station – remember WII FM? What's In It For Me? Because you've just told me what's in it for me when you told me your Fame Name®. And it's up to YOU to tell us. Don't leave it to other people…

Nicknames are not good

Because you may already have a Fame Name®. Yup. And if you don't yet have one for your Thing, you will. But if you don't choose it, it's called a nickname and this can backfire if you don't take charge.

To illustrate my point… I was speaking once at a great women's networking event and trotting through the theory of Fame Names when a lovely lady piped up and said 'I have one'. 'Great' I replied –

'what is it that you do?' 'I host parties where I sell Italian leather goods', 'Fab' I said, and what is your Fame Name®? 'Well… everyone calls me The Bag Lady' … ahh

As you can see, this can get a little lost in translation if you're now thinking of someone who has the misfortune to live on the streets with her possessions in a shopping trolley. Not quite the luxury leather goods image we want there…

An even better illustration (and this is a good example of how journalists can give you a nick name)… When I spoke once at a Hypnosis Conference I explained Fame Names as part of my talk, and afterwards a lovely chap came up to me at the drinks reception and told me he had a Fame Name®. Always excited to hear a new one, I asked what he did. Turns out he was an expert in using hypnosis to cure people of emetophobia (a fear of other people being sick). His Fame Name® was… Dr Vomit!

Now, this Fame Name® was working really well for him even though it was a nick name given by a journalist – he was getting PR and referrals for his expertise as a result. My point here though is that perhaps he would have preferred to come up with his own more palatable Fame Name® first. ☺

Zero competition

If you claim your Thing and set out a 'way' of describing it that's entirely yours, you set out your own market and therefore you have zero competition. Your Thing is *your* Thing and with the back-up of your philosophy there's nothing else quite like it. Monopoly time. Charge what you like, supply what you want, manage demand. Do it your way, as you like it.

One grain of sand

Your Fame Name® needs to be about your ONE THING 'boss' outcome. Not all the departments and sub-departments. We're not here to list out your CV of Thinging.

Imagine an hour glass. Every grain of sand is everything that you do, all the different ways of doing your Thing. They are all in there – departments, sub-departments, sub-sub-departments, etc. – but when they are all together it's hard to see what you do, they're all jumbled. There are lots and lots of elements to your Thinging, just like there are LOTS of grains of sand in an hour glass. You don't see an individual grain of sand clearly in an hour glass, apart from when it slips through the neck in the centre. THIS is why you need a Fame Name®: to define the one grain of sand that people see.

Don't talk about everything. Talk about THE THING! Your Fame Name® needs to be about the boss – that ultimate result you offer. Your Fame Name® tells us the transformation, result and outcome of you doing your Thing.

It doesn't have to be about you

The purpose of a Fame Name® is to get you noticed and remembered. It's a way of applying science to marketing to make your message stick. And if you don't want this to be about you, then use the Fame Name® process to name your business or your philosophy instead (this works just as well). Have a signature product or service that you're known for, but follow the principles of Fame Names to come up with what you're going to call that.

Run in parallel

Ideally, you want your Fame Name® to run in parallel with your actual name. Having a Fame Name® isn't about you creating a new identity. Instead, it's about harnessing the memory trick to get you and your Thing noticed. In time you'll be remembered for you (and your actual name!) but in the meantime, if you use a Fame Name® you'll get famous faster for your Thing. And then you can work on your ultimate goal…

The one-name Fame Name®!

You'll know you've made it when, like…

Elvis

Kylie

Madonna

Oprah

Branson

Obama

Beyoncé

you have just one name as your calling card (don't expect that to happen right away though!).

Here's exactly how you work out your Fame Name®. There are five elements of a Fame Name® (you might not use them all).

1. **Your transformation**

    This is the RESULT of your Thing, NOT your qualifications, your job title or your tools. You must must must make sure you talk about the transformation of your Thing, not the 'way' you do it and what the 'job' is that you do to get that result. So, you're not going to say you're an accountant or a website designer or a coach or a therapist. You'll say 'I help people to understand their business so it grows', or 'I help people sell more online', or 'I get people feeling confident', or 'I help people feel happy'.

NO JOB TITLES ALLOWED

I once told a roomful of hypnotherapists (100+ of them) that they weren't hypnotherapists – that was just their tool! What they DID was something else. The result and transformation of their hypnotherapy was their Thing. Something else entirely to the skill they all had. It's important to clearly explain the result of your Thing in your Fame Name®, as this is what people will buy (not how you do it).

2. **What's different?**

This is where you can own a market – set up your mini monopoly and eliminate competition. If you find a different way to explain your Thing, you'll instantly own that market. Because you invented it! Sounds simple? It is. So don't make it complicated. Don't get all cryptic and clever. Be simple, straightforward, perhaps take something well known and change the context, but don't get complicated. If you get complicated you'll cause confusion. And confused people never buy anything.

The lovely Dr Terry is The Skin Energy Doctor. She knows she's not the only anti-aging doctor around… Harley Street is pretty full of them for starters (and I'm sure there are a few thousand in LA). But Dr Terry is the only Skin Energy Doctor. See how simple that is – two ordinary everyday words, put into a different context, and you have your own market. Dr Terry now 'owns' the market of 'Skin Energy'. And she has the trademark™ on it too.

In fact I have the registered trademark ® for Fame Name®. So I 'own' that market.

When you say what is different about your Thing, you can create something of real value – IP. [For the uninitiated, IP is intellectual property – the name you call your Thing will build up a value of its own that you may one day want to sell (or licence, etc.). Building up IP around your Thing is a smart way to do business.]

So, give your Thing a name (and be different about it).

3. **Your position**

   You need to decide who you are when you do your Thing. You need to be clear about the role you play when you are doing your Thing.

Have a think. Are you a…

- cheerleader
- guide
- teacher
- arse-kicker (technical term!)
- leader
- commentator
- coach
- partner?

What's your *position* in relation to someone you're working with when you do your Thing? Work it out then put it in your Fame Name®. Find the right 'positioner' that tells us who you are to us (the people who need your Thing). Remember the 'What's In It For Me?' thing – well this is 'WHO are you to me?' When we're buying from someone – whether it's a product or a service – we want to know what role they are playing for us. Are they out front leading us, or bringing up the rear with a boot on our backside? Understand where you are and tell us.

Are you on top? Or at the side, or at the rear, or in a different pile? Know where you are in relation to your crowd with your Thing then reflect that in your Fame Name®. You might be a…

- queen
- guru
- expert
- architect
- teacher
- the… (i.e., the 'Go To') person
- manager.

This closes the scary gap. The gap between where you are right now (unknown or not known enough) and where you want to be (known for your Thing) can be closed in an instant by your Fame Name®. If you are being really clear about your position then you've staked your claim on your place in the market for your Thing.

Check in. If you choose a positioner and you're all good with it from the get go, it might be too comfortable. Go back and try harder. Because here's the deal, if you're not scared by your Fame Name® then it's probably not going to get you the visibility you need. If you don't have a sharp intake of breath when you come up with it, then chances are it won't cause a strong reaction in anyone else either. If you pick a 'cuddly'

Fame Name® you won't attract attention. If I was still a 'Marketing Consultant' instead of the 'Manager of Business Celebrities' that would frankly be quite dull – I certainly wouldn't be standing out. If The Flow Writer had been 'The write better books coach' it wouldn't be as powerful. If The Systems Superwoman had been 'The Systems Planner'... You see where I'm going with this? BOLDNESS is required.

The response you're looking for is this: 'who is THAT person and why do they think their Thing is all that, eh?' That's what's going to work for you. Make it scary and close that gap. Be bold and be a Business Celebrity! This is no time to be shy.

4. **Set out your market**

If you want to be clear about who you work with and who you don't (the latter being even more important), then make sure that's super-clear in your Fame Name® too. This is to stop you wasting your time. And it's to stop everyone else 'out there' who isn't after your Thing, and doesn't need what you do, wasting their time too. So if you only work with women, or dentists, or teenagers, or nutritionists, or parents or whoever it is your Thing is for, make that super-clear in your Fame Name®.

We already know you don't want to sell to people who don't have their hands up, so make it easy for those with them down to know that you're not for them! A Fame Name® offers you a clear shot direct into the market for your Thing, so don't aim everywhere.

5. **Personality fit**

A Fame Name® is not an opportunity for you to create a bizarre alter ego and hide behind it, however. Granted the alter ego thing will still work, because a Fame Name® will get you noticed. But at some point YOU will have to show up. For real. So best keep it authentic. And don't worry if you're not a razzamatazz person (I am a little bit but then that's just me). If you're quiet but purposeful, have a Fame Name® that matches that. If you're honest, direct and a little loud, have a Fame Name® that matches that (Diva works well here!). Be you, in all your glory, doing your Thing. That's the POINT!

Don't cross over to the Dark Side

Here's the deal. Fame Names work. I've seen it SO many times. And the science backs it up. These buggers work. And they work well. But my ask of you is that you use the force wisely, and don't convert to the Dark Side.

On the Dark Side you can invent a Fame Name® that will work for you like your best salesman 24/7. It will be out there getting you remembered and Googled like no-one's business. But If that isn't you *really* doing your Thing, and you know it's a persona you 'invented' because you thought it would work better, I ask you not to go there. The Dark Side doesn't win in the end (have you not seen the Death Star blow up? Twice!). Be authentic. It's easy to fake a Thing to market but not easy to sell it.

A close call with the Dark Side

Dave was very concerned about the Dark Side as he had been struggling with his sense of purpose and identity but was also turned off by a lot of people's marketing, talks and blogs and didn't want to 'be like that'. In fact, initially Dave was not even a fan of the idea of Being a Business Celebrity at ALL so even I was on his hit list! Dave and I got deeply into what it was specifically that was a problem for him, and discussed people whom he felt genuinely inspired by, and whose work he held in high esteem (luckily I made this cut). Dave admits this was a game-changing conversation for him as he realised just how important authenticity was to him.

With what he calls 'a highly tuned authenticity meter' (I'll be less polite and call it a bullsh*t detector!) Dave realised he was getting incredibly valuable feedback about how he did and didn't want to do his Thing. When you're following other people's models of success without using everything you've learned it's difficult to do your own Thing. Dave had worked in some HUGE name corporate businesses before working independently but still within a business coaching franchise, so had been inside other people's Things (some of which he liked and some he didn't!). Now Dave saw exactly how to be his own Indie Professional and it was everything to do with being authentic. His business is called Sleeping Tiger. It's absolutely who Dave is.

Find the right words

You need to spend time on your Fame Name®. Play with words. Your Thesaurus is your friend! If you get the meaning but a word is not right, your Fame Name® won't quite fit. Like your Thing fits you perfectly, so will your Fame Name®. So when you're close, have a rummage around the edges of the words you have already. Find alternatives that might fit better. Don't settle and don't try to make something fit that isn't you.

The A list and the B list

What you'll have from this process is a list of words that covers the five elements of a Fame Name®. Now it's going to be a pretty long Fame Name® if it has ALL those elements in it (probably), so rank them.

- Have A list words.
- Have B list words.

And that's okay because you have somewhere else to use them…

- Add on a strap.

Adding a 'strapline' to your Fame Name® will anchor it, strengthen it and make it stick even more. And this is where you can use your 'leftover' words. If there are any words on your A list (and B list) that don't make it into your Fame Name®, get them into strapline. This adds to your positioning.

My strapline is 'Find your Thing and get Famous for it', so you know that as a 'Manager of Business Celebrities' that is my role – it's the getting famous for your Thing, not anything else. Your strapline is there to remove any ambiguity about what you and your Thing are about. Make it super-clear what your Thing is and who you do it for. Otherwise you'll be 'talking' to the wrong crowd.

What to do with your Fame Name® when you have it

Here are some ideas to make your Fame Name® work for you:

- get its URL (website address) or at least have a web page that gets found if someone searches on your Fame Name®;
- get a Facebook page/Twitter profile/whatever social media you use of it;
- have it on your name badge (at networking, events, in the street?!);
- state it in your bio (the one you have on your website and at the end of press releases);
- explain it when you tell your story (read the next chapter for more on that);
- start conversations with it (these may lead to sales);

(*continued*)

- use it as your book title (yes, I am sure you have a book in you);
- demand it as your speaker intro! – you want to show up on stage with your Fame Name® (same goes for journalists writing articles about you);
- sign off your emails with it (you send a lot of those I'm sure);
- be it! – you have to own your Fame Name® by showing up as you doing your Thing. You are that person (oh yes).

'I don't need one'

I hear you cry. A Fame Name® is a bit silly isn't it? Well… You don't have to have one, as it's only a marketing tool. BUT… not having a Fame Name® can mean your position isn't clear. Your Thing isn't clear. We don't know what you do that's different. We can't quite tell if we need you or not. Remember, you want a decision. Don't let people umm and ahh when they meet you (or meet your marketing). Make it super-clear what you do and if it's something they need. Do you solve their problem – YES OR NO? That's all you need to do in your marketing to make it successful, make yourself clear.

Business Celebrity Marmite tastes good

As the catchphrase goes, you either Love or Hate Marmite, and while I'd prefer you didn't incite feelings of hatred, you do want this reaction. By having a Fame Name® you will instantly connect – or not – with people. You'll be so clear on what it is that you do – and don't do – that 'they' will know too. There will be no waffle. No 'hmm, what exactly is that?' It will be obvious. Black and white. Totally clear. The only question people will need to answer is 'Am I in or am I out?' And if they're in, then you can do your Thing.

Chapter 5

INTERESTING STORIES SELL

You need to tell us the WHY of your Thing, because we will buy your 'why'. It's all the details 'we' (the royal buying public 'we') want to know to help us see clearly that you are THE person we want to do business with. Whether your business is just you or you are the spokesperson or figurehead – we want to buy from you.

Don't be faceless

This is a mistake. No matter how big your business, it needs a face. It needs an identity and a set of values. And these don't appear from nowhere – they are part of a story. We want to get to KNOW you so we can LIKE you and then we'll TRUST you, which means we'll BUY from you. It's an often-quoted process but not everyone knows how to do it – because they leave out the story.

Everyone is interesting

I say that 'interesting stories sell' and I will follow that up with a swift EVERYONE IS INTERESTING before you insist that you're not. Just because you don't think your own story is interesting doesn't mean that it isn't. People love detail, they love history, they love to get to know you. I'm sure you've read an autobiography, or watched a 'fly-on-the-wall' documentary, or even got to know someone by asking about their life. Of course you have.

We're all nosey

Humans are nosey. And that's okay, it's who we are. We need to know if we can trust people and we definitely want to know if they understand us. Everyone wants to be understood, so if we can find out more about you and see the connection of empathy or sympathy, we're sold. Literally. We're there with our money and buying from you. We're tuning into that radio station again – WII FM (What's In It For Me?). We like to buy from someone who 'gets' us. We don't want to be sold to, we want someone to understand our problem THEN solve it. Not just shove a solution at us! This is why you must tell the story of your Thing.

Once upon a time...

I am not suggesting that you need to write your autobiography, but we do want to know your life triggers. What events, thoughts, moments, conversations and ideas triggered you into doing your Thing? What signposts can you give us along the way so we get that you get us? We want to buy in to you (again, literally) so let us in.

You were there

The reason you may not see or appreciate your story as interesting is of course that you were there at the time. You already know what happened! And like small children growing up, when you see them every day you don't notice how tall they've got but take them to an Aunty who's not seen them for a while and they've shot up! Ha, how did THAT happen? It's not magic. It's just what is. BUT you need to pick out the poignant pieces, the parts of your story that show us how you got to your Thing today.

Don't forget your 'why-nots'

Not only do we want to know why you do what you do, but we also want to know why you *don't* do what you don't do. Your Thing is very clear and you don't do it for everyone (skip back a couple of chapters if you've not sorted that out yet!). Part of your story of working out your Thing will also account for the decisions you made along the way to *not* do what you don't do. There will be situations you won't work in, or problems you don't solve. These are just as important as the 'whys' as they point us to even more clarity about your Thing. Don't leave them out!

There's more than one way to tell a story

I'm not going to pretend to be a story-telling expert, but to help you see how this works I'll walk you through a few threads. The key is remembering (and being happy that) your story is your story and it might not fit a formula perfectly. This is not an exercise in filling in the blanks. Your story may be a farm full of fables, or a mash-up of meanderings. I don't know, but you do. What you need to know is that it's important to tell it. Style is less important than substance.

What your story needs to tell us

For me, there are five factors to stories that sell...

- trust
- credibility
- experience
- qualifications
- and last but absolutely not least, telling the TRUTH.

All these elements are linked. You'll create trust by telling the truth. You'll sound credible if you share with us the ups *and* downs. There will be highs of experience and lows too. We want to know you're qualified so we can trust your expert opinion, but don't worry if your experience *is* your qualification. You might not need certificates as the 'hours' count, as do testimonials. Wrap all these elements up together into YOUR STORY.

No-one is expecting it all to be sugar coated with only shiny happy people in it, as let's be honest we like a nice bit of doom and gloom to add contrast. ☺ Nothing says 'fake story' like a perfect fairy tale.

The best stories aren't yours

The best stories you can tell aren't even your own – they are of the people you have done your Thing with/to/for. Client stories – testimonials and case studies – are the best stories you can have to help you get famous for your Thing. Even if you're just starting out with a brand new Thing, I'll bet you have some examples of you doing your Thing (even if it's in a different context or you weren't charging for it at the time). You can also 'borrow' stories – BE CAREFUL here as I am not saying you should take other people's stories. What I am saying is you can take stories that show the 'Thing you do' working. So if you have a technique you use, or there is evidence you can share, even if you didn't do it yourself, then that's a story you can use too.

Sharing science is a good example of borrowing a story. I do it with Fame Name® (the Baker/baker paradox). That's a story of how 'it' (i.e., my Thing) works, even though it's not about me doing it. Add your angle and the story is yours.

Connection is key

The purpose of telling the story of your Thing is connection. Connection is the special sauce that helps you to sell. There is a reason why big brands spend a fortune on story telling (in the form of advertising and PR) – it's all about connection. The reason the Apple store has queues outside when it's a new release day? Connection. We all want to belong. This is caveman stuff. Back in prehistoric times we all wanted to be in the tribe otherwise we'd have been eaten. And even now, we want to be connected and part of something. So, people need to know your story to buy in to you, join your tribe and then buy from you. Make sure your story is FOR your audience and builds your connection with your crowd.

This is the point of it. You'll do your Thing anyway, but if you want people to buy your Thing, get connected to them. Story telling is a smart way to get connected and is brilliant content for wider broadcasts (as you can't meet everyone personally).

One at a time

Having said that you can't meet everyone personally, you still need to tell your story as if it's one to one. It's never a 'broadcast', hoping someone will pick up the frequency. When you're telling your story (just like with all of your marketing), remember you are telling ONE person about your Thing. You are talking to ONE person, not a crowd. Just like I am typing this for you now. I'm not writing for everyone, I'm writing for you… because you're reading this right now.

Always remember that your Thing is an answer to a problem, and always speak ONLY to the person you know has the problem. You might have the 'conversation' 1000 times but you have each one, one at a time.

When you connect, people get you.

When they get you, they get your Thing.

If your Thing is what they need, they get it.

They buy.

Everyone's happy.

Empathy, sympathy and understanding

Your story needs to connect through empathy, sympathy and understanding. If you've 'been there', talk about it and empathise with people. And if you've not been there personally, then sympathise instead. You don't need to have experienced the same problem that you now solve with your Thing. But if you have, make sure that's clear in your story. If you do your Thing because you got so annoyed about something you had to fix it, that's a clear case of sympathy. When your audience knows that you understand them, they'll be connected and your story will be selling for you.

How to zest a story

Rachel is a great example of an 'I've been where you are now' story. When she shares her 'fat photo' (sorry Rachel, there's no nice way to put that!) and explains that this was her 'then' and then shows her 'gorgeous zesty lady' picture (slimmer, brighter, totally fabulous) there are usually audible gasps from her audience. The gasps get louder when she adds that the 'fat photo' is Rachel in her 30s looking a *lot* older than her 'this is me now picture', which is Rachel in her 50s (looking 30-something). Yeah she's been there – stressed out, overweight, not sleeping, junk-food-fuelled, jet set job, hating what she saw in the mirror. Fast forward (via various triggers) she is now vibrant, voracious (for life), eats amazingly well (including gourmet food), fighting fit and flexible too (that will be the yoga), and devoted to helping other people 'just like the old her' get zesty. By sharing her journey of transformation we see how her 'zest lifestyle' Thing is now taking her passion for feeling fabulous to people who have their hands up to the problems she had. Empathy in spades, and connection instantly if you are that person.

Here are some story shapes

Forget fairy tales – fantasy stories are 'Dark Side' marketing. Stories absolutely work as little sales people beavering away on your behalf, but pick a good TRUE one. Untrue stories will leave you unstuck. And without sales.

You the hero

You finding your Thing might be you being a hero. This is the 'best seller' of stories. The hero's journey is well told and instantly recognisable. Think *Star Wars*, *Harry Potter* and *Superman*. These are all hero journeys. There's good versus evil, the baddies nearly win but the goodies triumph in the end. There are obstacles along the way and it looks like winning is impossible, but through twists and turns the hero makes it out on top. Phew. The world didn't end. There are ups and downs. But eventually good triumphs and the Thing is found.

This is a legend story, where you as the hero fought your way through the thicket before the Thing was found in the clearing. There was struggle and near disaster but you persevered and eventually the breakthrough came. You have your Thing. You're a hero. You might not have a super-dramatic version of this story, but you might have a slice of it. I know I do. There was no 'living in a skip' for me, going from penniless to perfectly happy doing my Thing. Having said that, there have definitely been some ups and downs and twists and turns. These don't have to be enormous to be interesting. You might even, like I did, feel guilty for having really quite a nice life, nothing actually (from the outside) to grumble about, but still disgruntled that you didn't have your Thing yet… feeling a little 'spoilt child' about the whole thing. And that can make it even harder to then go do your Thing because 'what's all that about?', surely you can't be that ungrateful for what you have. Been there. ☺

Just tell your story. Look at your journey and pick out the tricky bits. If you're only just working out your Thing now, there will be a story before. It's never straightforward. Your Thing can be hard to see, so there's bound to be something you can write about the 'fog' beforehand. It might not be a big dramatic movie (series) yet but it will have struggle, no matter how small. There's always a story. And it's always real (therein lies connection, lest we forget).

Reluctant?

You may be a reluctant hero. Rather than being on a mighty quest, you may have felt you had no choice. I felt like this. I was quite happy sitting quietly at home, doing my marketing thing, not bothering too many people. But then I got annoyed (as you know). I could see all these people with brilliant Things that seemed to be invisible to them. Something needed to be done, and no-one else was doing anything! Why wasn't anyone telling them? What was THAT all about?

It was so obvious what needed doing (more personality in your marketing people!) that I eventually, and somewhat hesitantly (after all, it involved me making somewhat of a spectacle of myself), stepped up and started doing my Thing. My Thing was just too much to ignore. I put on my cape, reluctantly (although not without adding a few sequins to it first, of course!)...

I'm not the only one

Jennifer felt like this too. After seeing her Thing in all its glory (I had a hand in that!) she had a sense of herself, her strengths and her contribution to the world that had been invisible in all but the moments of a client's key achievements. And then it seemed too much. Jennifer is not here to make a small impact – her vision and mission are HUGE (think global and not just in this dimension).

It took Jennifer a while (several months in fact) to really get that it had to be her doing this Thing. This was her Thing and it was important. And only after that time of reflection did she have the confidence to take what she calls her 'nuttiness' out into the world and introduce it to new people, along with a vision of the awe-inspiring and potent world they could create with their companies.

You can see how, when your Thing is big, new, different or just 'something else', it's easy to become reluctant, but you must still be the hero… The world is waiting.

Compelled!

It might be that you had a compulsion (not to be confused with a convulsion!) when you found your Thing. When you realised what your Thing is and what you can do, your 'why' compelled you into action. This happens a lot when people realise their Thing is a cause or a crusade. This is how charities get started and movements get moving.

If your story led you towards something *so* compelling that you had to…

DROP

EVERYTHING

AND

DO

IT

NOW

then that's what you have to tell us. This is a really energising type of story and gets us excited about you and your Thing. We can feel the intensity and passion in a compelling story – so whatever you do, don't tone it down!

Lost and found?

Maybe you've been lost... lost in the search for your Thing or lost looking for an answer. And now you've found it you want to share it, do it, be it, make it. As you tell a lost-and-found story you'll have people rooting for you. They'll jump straight into your tribe and get involved, because they'll either see that where you're heading is towards them, or towards the answer they need. Talk about what it was like to be lost and how great it is now you're found. This is case study gold, and a direct line to connection and trust.

Mistakes? I've made a few...

We've all made some. Even those of us who are practically perfect in every way. ☺ So your story might be about mistakes you made and what you did about them. Or maybe you only realised you'd made mistakes some time after they happened. Whenever and whatever the mistakes were, we're making the assumption that where you are now (i.e., doing your Thing) is NOT a mistake. We want to learn from your mistakes and hear what you learnt from them too. And anyone who can own up to making mistakes is instantly credible, assumed to be truthful – so we'll be connected right away.

Did you invent this?

Are you an inventor? Did you create something brand new when you worked out your Thing? Is what you do so easy but so different that it's brand new? Did getting grumpy unleash the mad inventor in you? If it did, tell us! If you were so annoyed by something that you invented your Thing as an answer to it, we want to hear about that. We want to hear how you invented it. We want to understand the thought processes and the steps you took.

If you always asked questions like 'How can I make this quicker, better, smarter, smoother, clearer?' you're probably an inventor. If all or part of your story is that you're a fixer, tell us the fixes (the ones that worked and *more importantly* the ones that didn't). Definitely tell us about all the failures you had along the way in your 'lab'. Yes of course we'll buy the one that works from you now you've worked out your Thing, but we'll buy with even more certainty if we know all the ways that didn't work too (not to mention we won't bother trying them either!).

Was it your destiny?

Perhaps you've always known you'd be doing your Thing one day. Maybe you always had that feeling… that there was something else for you to do. Do you have that? Feel that you're here to do something bigger, with more impact? Stand out – get noticed – maybe even be famous as a Business Celebrity? And it's not about EGO! This isn't about showing off and thinking thoughts that are 'above you'. There is nothing above you (only sky!)…

Yes, I am having a woo woo moment but why not? Not everything can be explained in logical terms when it comes to your story. Some things just didn't 'feel right' for me. Sometimes I 'just knew' I wasn't in the right place. Maybe you've had those feelings too – that gut feel or intuition – knowing that somewhere you have a Thing to do (and it's not what you're doing right now). It's just Destiny calling… Hello? Hello? Is it me you're looking for?

It's not all or nothing

All these story shapes aren't meant to be a choose-one-over-the-other option. You can have elements of all of them, some of them, none of them in YOUR story. Your story is your story and it's not all or nothing, it's whatever happened on the journey to your Thing. It's the truth.

You know your story

I know you know your story. It's not new for you. But don't leave anything out. Very often (in fact this happens almost every time I do this with someone) there will be a part of your story that you think is 'not interesting' or 'not relevant' and this is almost always the JUICIEST, most interesting, most compelling, most exciting part of your story – the part that will create the most connection. Do not leave out the 'odd' bits of your story, as it's always the trivia that sticks.

Make it sticky

If your Fame Name® is like a Post-it note, your story is like superglue on a billboard. The ultimate purpose of your story is to stick. It needs to stick to sell for you. People need to remember you, so they can refer to you, or Google you, or file you away for when they need you. You tell your story to add to the stickiness of your message and marketing. And guess what? Teeny tiny details stick the best. Just like those seeds that get stuck in your teeth, it's the tiniest little flavoursome details of stories that stick. And niggle. And work their way in so there's no chance they'll be forgotten. There is a lot of skill in story telling (not all of which I've mastered), but I can tell you now, the detail is what will sell for you. Make yourself as sticky as you possibly can, it can only be a good thing for your Thing.

Your story is your message

You need to share your story because it's a fundamental part of your marketing. It's the core of your marketing in fact. All those hours you could waste 'coming up with' a USP (Unique Selling Point) you don't need to.

You have a PSP

A Personality Selling Point. Hooray – hours of brainstorming not required for this. If you make your message and your marketing all about you, then it's automatically unique. Your story is yours. It's your view of the world and how it happened to you. Your story is how you arrived at doing your Thing. It's an insight into how you think and how you work. It's the way you connect so you get clients.

Make all your marketing sit around your message, even if it's a mess!

There's nothing wrong with a mess as long as you put signposts in so we can follow you through it.

Where to use your story

- Absolutely have it on your website.
- Your 'About' page needs to be about you – this is the showcase for your story.
- Tell people what they need to know about you to get connection. Make it as long or as short as you need. There are NO RULES!
- Speak your story – share it on stage, in interviews, on the radio, wherever you have an audience.
- Wherever you MEET YOUR MARKET you need to tell your story.
- Why would you not share your best sales person? Get them selling for you!
- Your story builds connection.
- All that's left for people to do once they hear your story is to decide yes or no to whether your Thing is something they need.

Your 'why' is why we buy from you

So tell us your story – otherwise we don't know why to buy.

Chapter 6

NOTHING IS IMPOSSIBLE

This is the mindset bit. To really DO your Thing you have to BELIEVE in your Thing, which most of the time will mean you need to believe in you. There's only so much I can tell someone about their Thing before I have to wait and see if they 'do it', because that 'sitting at home on your own being amazing' thing is a very real option. It can be scary to finally find your Thing and realise how BIG it is. Even when you've wanted something for a long time, when you get it you can still freak out. I see it all the time. I do it myself. I even freaked out over this book deal and went quiet on the publishers. Yes I know it's daft, but it's what we do when we get what we want. Sometimes we don't think we deserve it, or it can't be that easy.

Obviously I had to remind myself of my own stuff – your Thing *is* easy, and yes you have to believe in it. And of course I didn't run away and hide for ever as if I had there would be no book for you to read now. Doesn't mean I didn't have a wobble though...

It's like the trapeze

I'd always wanted to be able to swing on the trapeze. Or do something equally dare devil. I once had a mentor who used the metaphor of letting go of one trapeze before you can swing to the other to describe how sometimes you have to let go and leap before you catch the next thing. So there I was one day in LA with time on my hands (as you do) – I'd actually flown over for an event to do some more learning – and the flight back to London didn't leave until the evening. So there I was thinking 'hmm, what shall I do' when I remembered (you know those sticky details in a story – well, that) my trapeze-fan mentor said she'd learnt to trapeze in LA. I'm not sure if you've been to LA but suffice to say it's a pretty big city. Of course in my naivety (or was it intuition?) I was convinced the trapeze school would be in Santa Monica where I was staying. And I was sure she had said it was on the beach… so off I strolled from the hotel, along a few blocks to the beach with this trapeze thing half on my mind. Because I knew if I saw the trapeze school I'd have to do it! Ever make deals like that with yourself? I do it all the time…

So I was both relieved and annoyed when I'd walked all the way to Santa Monica pier and there was no sign of a trapeze school. On the one hand the relief was very real (phew, no need to do death-defying stunts today as the trapeze looks very scary) and on the other hand I was a little bit disappointed (that I couldn't do any death-defying stunts today even though they scared me silly). I made another deal with myself. I'd walk to the end of the pier and back then head to the shops for some retail therapy and lunch (what is it about piers that you have to walk to the end?). So I'm midway through my stroll and there it is, the trapeze school is only on the bloody pier. So of course I got right on it…

Ha ha. No I didn't. I panicked and had words with myself. I stood at the fence and watched. And watched...

'Go on, you know you want to do it, just go do it.'

'Nooo, have you seen how high up they are? It doesn't look safe to me!'

'But you made a deal with yourself that if you saw the trapeze school you'd do it.'

'Ah but that was if I saw it on the beach – this is the pier – that's entirely different...'

'You don't even know if they have space on a class yet, surely you can just go and ask?'

'Ah but if they do have a space it will be embarrassing to say no thanks'.

'GET IN THE OFFICE AND ASK THEM!'

Yes I was stood there watching and having a chat with myself about actually doing the thing that I knew I wanted to do but was talking myself out of. How many times have you done that? Don't worry, you can keep it to yourself if it's a big number!

I asked

After a decent period of observation (!) I went into the office to at least see if I could learn to trapeze that day. Unfortunately (?) the group/class they had on was about to finish and the next one wasn't until later that afternoon, which would have meant cutting it fine for the airport. Oh well, at least I'd asked. And then the Universe had the last laugh. 'Oh but hang on...' were the scariest words to come out of a trapeze school front desk person ever...

'They only had a small group this morning and they'll be done in a few minutes and the guys are on the clock until 12:30. You could take up the time one to one if you wanted to.'

'Uh-huh I gulped.'

Ten minutes later I'm in a harness and wearing a brand new pair of socks, having spent nine of the previous ten minutes initialing a very long and detailed disclaimer (this was the USA after all, and I was about to do something death-defying). So, I had precisely one minute for any rational thoughts about what I was about to do. And then it hit me. What the hell was I doing? I have small people! No-one knows I am here! There is absolutely no need in the world for me to do this! I am so selfish! I am so crazy! Helpppppp…

I didn't hear a word he said

When I was led out to my lovely instructor all I could see was his mouth moving and various arm gestures up to the VERY HIGH UP AND VERY TINY board I was supposed to climb a VERY TALL LADDER to. I didn't hear a word! So I said (and this is good advice for any situation, including business I think), 'I didn't get all of that. Could you please tell me what I need to do when I need to do it, one step at a time.'

I thought I could handle that.

I was wrong!

There's always another way

I would love to tell you I trotted up that incredibly tall ladder and swung with the greatest of ease and did a back flip on the way down. Instead, my feet transfixed themselves to that tiny (very high up) platform and the idea of leaning out (leaning out?! Are you mad!) to grab the trapeze was not going to happen. In my head I felt I was reaching out perpendicularly to the platform but in reality I was MILES away from reaching the trapeze. Ha. They make it look so easy… casually leaning out to grab the trapeze. Nonchalant, that's the word I'm looking for. Must be their Thing…

Anyway, there I am NOT reaching the trapeze so we switch to plan B.

Plan B is a bear hug

Here we try a different approach. The instructor is now bear hugging me around the waist, allowing me to reach out without freaking out. Another 'trapezer' trots (and she really does) up the very tall ladder and reaches out to get the trapeze for me. Finally, I am holding the trapeze in my hands.

I hold on

You'd think at this point I'd have 'decided' I was going to do this. You'd think I'd have committed to swinging on the trapeze while teetering on the edge of a tiny platform at the top of a very tall ladder. But no, I am still having THAT conversation with myself:

'Why do this?!'

'Why not?'

Rinse and repeat.

It hurt more to hold on than let go

And so I let go.

And I flew.

And I loved it.

If you head over to the book's website I'll make sure you can see the mad grin I had on my face when I finally flew through the air with the greatest of ease. Apparently I was right… nothing is impossible. I also learnt something else important.

Always have an exit plan!

Let's just say my dismount was less than stylish… But style doesn't matter! It's only substance that counts.

How's your state of mind?

What deals are you making with yourself about your Thing? Without you 'getting' this – that nothing is impossible – the rest of this process won't work. Or it might work a little bit, but you won't own nearly as much as you can and you won't do as much with it as you could.

Time to decide

Are you really going to do your Thing? Up to you. You can easily do every step up to now, on your own, keeping it to yourself. But now you have to decide. Are you going to share it? Are you going to go out there and get famous for it? It's not about finding it and making the plan, it's about DOING THE PLAN… You've done all the easy bits now (really) and we need to have a chat with the you in your head.

Hello, are you in there?

I want your 'little voice' to hear this part now. Make sure you're letting them. If you're all good with your personal development you'll whizz through this chapter. If you've never had that conversation with yourself it's a chapter you'll want to make sure you read carefully.

Don't stop in your tracks

You have it all now – where to find your Thing, what to do with it when you have it, what to call it (or you) and how to make your message sticky with stories. But now it's for REAL. This can be a hurdle. It might even be a brick wall.

Don't overthink it

Don't even think about it at all. Your Thing is your Thing and you need to do it. End of. Ah! If only it were that simple… If, right now, you're having a back-and-forth conversation in your head about doing or not doing your Thing, about stepping out with a Fame Name®, about who on earth would want to buy anything from you, let alone the thing you just realised was your Thing that you're not even (**gasp**) qualified in. Read on…

You need to get over it

You need to feel it to make it happen. Believe it. Know it. Own it. Do it. You already *are* a Business Celebrity. The question is, do you believe that?

If you can think it, you can do it

I'm getting serious now. Because I know if you don't really get this, if you don't really own this, the rest of it won't work as well as it can. You'll do okay, but will you be committed and have people commit to you? Maybe not…

Don't think like this...

I can't do it!

Who am I to think I can do this Thing?

Everyone will laugh at me!

I'm not ready.

I'm not good enough.

I just need to get this perfect before...

I'll do it next week/month/year/blue moon.

You're not on your own. I've heard them all before (in my own head and from other people!). As Tom Jones would warble – it's not unusual... But you can ignore them. If you want to do your Thing, you can choose the thoughts you want to listen to. And I'd suggest you give all the above a swerve if you want to get in your spotlight. We all ask these questions. What really matter are the answers.

Give yourself some good answers

Yes, you can!

You're you – and that's what we want!

Yes, some people might laugh at your Thing, but some might cry – with joy!

You'll never be 100% ready – I hate to break that to you (there's always another level to take it to!) but as long as you can have a go now, have a go now.

Forget getting it perfect... it's never going to happen. So get over it. If you do your best it will be perfect for right now.

Stop procrastinating. If you can do it next week you can do it now. So do it! Better it gets finished than it never sees the light of day…

I am a professional procrastinator, so I set deadlines for myself. I make all my products and events live. I'd never 'get around to them' if they stayed on the to-do list. And don't think I didn't make myself publicly accountable (Facebook is a wonderful thing) to get this book written on time. Deadlines are my magic trick. Work out yours.

There are lots of ways to believe in you

The following ideas are just some that I know about and I encourage you to find what works for you. The aim of the exercise is to get you believing in yourself so you deal with your 'stuff' in a way that makes sense for you. Actually it doesn't even have to make sense – it just needs to work! Everyone has stuff… find a fix that works for you.

Some people swear by affirmations

Write down or say out loud or read, every day, something that makes you confident and excited to do your Thing. A simple one is 'I am good enough' or 'My Thing is brilliant and needed in the world'. Post it on the mirror/fridge/kettle/loo door… anywhere you see it all the time. If you've not tried it, give it a go. It works for a lot of people.

Have a vision

Make a vision board, have visual reminders of what it will look like when you do your Thing. Have images that show you how you know it can be. The visuals can remind you *why* you do your Thing, what it will look like when you do your Thing. It might show you on a stage, it might show a bank statement for your Thing business account. Be clear, be specific but VISUALIZE it. Did you know that your mind has no filter between what's real and what's imagined? So you can trick it… sneaky!

Set your sights on a target

Targets work. Write them down. Go public with them. There's a lot to be said for sharing your targets in making them real. Accountability is a wonderful thing! Have a number or measure that you can track against. I do this all the time with the number of people I want to welcome at my events or work with on a certain course. Or the number of words I want to write before a deadline… ahem.

Have a goal

Go towards it… If it's a big enough goal then it will draw you towards it. Not big enough (or juicy enough) and it might not have any effect. So choose wisely, and make the goal yours.

Too often I see people pick a goal off the shelf – a one-size-fits-all goal. Do you actually want a Ferrari? (I don't, Aston Martin maybe but not a Ferrari thanks.) Do you want to live in a mansion? (No thanks, I'd rather have four different beach houses around the world.) Do you want rails of designer clothes? (Have you met my children? Having posh clothes with sticky fingers around would be a waste of time…) Do you want a butler to pack your suitcases then unpack and press your clothes when you arrive on a business trip? (Well maybe… ☺)

Pick out your goals, and make them ones you're connected to. I have goals around influence and impact. I want to help a large number of people find their Thing. I want to contribute to charities and have an impact on how we all do business. I don't want to work in the school holidays, instead I want to go on adventures with my children, showing them the world. These are MY goals. What are YOUR goals?

You may want to step away

Often we're more motivated by 'away-from' goals. It's sometimes easier to see and say what we absolutely don't want. I absolutely don't want a job! I absolutely don't want to commute, or waste any of my time doing things I don't want to. My away-from goals are quite clear. But they are now part of my life. I've made my life work that way (plus I honestly don't think anyone would actually hire me to do a proper job!). If you're looking to find your Thing to 'get away' from where you are right now, 'away-from' goals will work. Make sure they are big and hairy so you don't want to be anywhere near them! We're all more likely to take action to stop something, or fix something that's broken than move towards something 'nice'. It's just how we work as humans. Sometimes we'll even wait until things actually break… Not advised. Do it now. Set the goal. Move away before it gets too bad!

Thoughts become Things

I am sure you've heard this before. What you think becomes your reality. If you wake up in a bad mood, guess what? You'll probably have a bad day. You thought it up. You'll only spot the bad in your day even if there is good in there too, because YOU decided it was going to be a bad day. You'll see what you're thinking. Yes, of course 'bad stuff' happens, but it's how you deal with it that makes the difference. If you allow your thoughts to take over, you *will* turn into the grumpy person who believes they can't do their Thing.

If you've got this far, and said you want to find your Thing, looked at your easy and your annoying, worked out a Fame Name®, put your story together and NOW you decide you can't do it… I can pretty much guarantee you'll be annoyed. Grumpy in fact. And you'll have created that grumpiness. But that also means…

- If your thoughts become things then you just need to THINK YOUR THING.

- If you think you can do your Thing, you can.
- If you decide people will buy your Thing, they will.
- Think your Thing into existence and it will be there.

Magic tricks of the mind…

It's only thinking

We have 60–80,000 thoughts a day. That's a lot I think (ha ha). I'd be impressed if all the thoughts you have are positive and about doing your Thing. There's going to be all sorts of thoughts in there – from practical bodily function-related ones to existential ones, to supportive ones and those unhelpful negative ones. You don't have to listen to all of them. Just say 'next!' Take notice of the thoughts you want to take notice of. Or don't take notice of any of them and just do your Thing anyway. Entirely up to you. They're not real things, they're just thoughts.

Turn yourself inside out

There's an approach to thinking about thinking based on these three principles:

- mind
- consciousness
- thought.

I do not profess to fully 'get' inside-out thinking (and actually the point is not to get it but just not to do any thinking), but I have some amazing clients and friends who swear by this approach to non-thinking – it's worth knowing about. When you realise your Thing is your Thing, and whatever you think about it are just thoughts, you are then free to just do it. It might take you a little while to get your head around that (or rather not get your head around that), but can you see how not thinking about your Thing will allow you to do it without any thoughts (negative or positive) about it? Just do it for the sake of doing it and suspend all thoughts 'about' it.

Don't think

Give yourself a head break. Go for a walk, or swim or meditate. Find your 'quiet place' and let clarity sneak in the back door when you're not thinking. This is when you'll find all the good stuff about your Thing. If you have any questions about your Thing, know that you have the answers already… you just have to shut up your head chatter so you can hear them. Yes I know that's super woo-woo, but it's just how it is. And if you 'know' about the importance of taking quiet time but aren't 'doing' it, then find the time. Most of the reasons why you don't do your Thing will be outside noise – influences and thinking – that comes from stuff happening 'outside' of you instead of inside you. If it's raining, that's not a sign your Thing's not going to work. It's just raining. If the economy is down (or up), it's nothing to do with your Thing. If someone else says something to you that makes you 'feel' you can't do your Thing. Guess what… ignore them. It's outside out of your control. Only you control your Thing – ON THE INSIDE.

You create your Thing

You need to think your Thing into existence and then it will be there. Just like that. You decide what to think about it, how to share it, who to offer it to and every other decision that needs to be made. It's your Thing. You're in charge.

Being fearless doesn't mean no fear

It just means you don't think 'badly' about the fear. In fact, you might get to the point where you look for things that scare you as then you know they are important… I still get nervous when I work with people one to one, or speak to a big crowd. I am nervous because I want it to have an impact, I want to make sure I do my Thing and deliver the result of clarity. I am nervous about it not working. I'm not nervous of doing it; instead I just want to have a great result happen. The point is, I *always* do my Thing, fear or no fear.

Protect your spotlight

Only you can do your Thing. You need to be connected to YOU to make your Thing work. You can 'do' Being a Business Celebrity or you can 'be' a Business Celebrity. There is a massive difference. One is where you just follow a process and a formula and get some different marketing for your business. The other (being) is where you put YOU in the process and BE a Business Celebrity – in your thoughts and your Thing. You put YOU out there and connect with the people that need you and your Thing. There's only room in your spotlight for you and nothing else. So the clearer you are on your Thing, with clear thoughts and connection, the stronger you'll stand out.

But it's not about you

Remember that your Thing is not for you, it's for the people who need it. It might be your thinking but your Thing is not about you.

- You're only ever one thought away from impossible to possible.
- You're only ever one thought away from doing your Thing.
- You're only ever one thought away from your spotlight.

But you need to think it into existence…

You're an artist

Be creative. Do your art. Dream and experiment and do your Thing! Make it, record it, write it, do it. SHIP IT! Get your Thing out into the world so that you have a legacy – a legacy that's 100% yours, not borrowed. Just because no-one's done it that way before doesn't mean it won't sell. If you solve a problem that needs solving – ship it. Choose your subject well, choose the right people to work with and do your Thing with. Like an artist, get in your flow (which will mean not overthinking).

Have certainty

It's one thing to know what your Thing is, but it's entirely another to be certain about it. You have to be absolutely certain about what you do and why you do it. You NEED to feel like this and you WILL feel like this if it is your Thing. Know the benefits of your Thing – read your testimonials, remind yourself how brilliant you are. If you've got out of Thinging mode this can flip you back into it superfast. And stop any thoughts that aren't helping. Connect with the benefits you bring, connect with who you help.

Feel the connection

That's when you'll know you're doing your Thing.

Don't put up a fence

There is NO LIMIT to how big your Thing can get. So don't put up a barrier or a fence around it when there isn't one. It's not up to you to put fences up. If they are needed they'll be there (maybe because of culture or language) but don't box yourself in to be smaller than you are. Go international if you want to – all you need to do is take away the fences.

You choose

You get to choose exactly how you do your Thing, where you do it, who you do it with, what you say about it, where you say it, what it looks like, how big (or small) it is… You choose everything about your Thing and your business, including how you think about it – so choose wisely.

Be amazing

- Doing your Thing makes you feel amazing.
- You doing your Thing makes who you help feel amazing.
- It's all about the amazing.
- The only thought you need: *Do your Thing*.

Chapter 7

GET IN YOUR SPOTLIGHT

This is it. We've finally got to the real marketing part of you doing your Thing. This is the final piece in the puzzle of doing your Thing and getting paid for it. Because without getting in your spotlight no-one is going to know about you, and if they don't know about you then they can't get your Thing, which of course isn't going to help anyone.

There's a reason this comes at the end of the sequence. If you jump straight to the 'spotlight' stuff then you're just doing marketing of some-thing, not necessarily your Thing thing. Not that there is anything wrong with 'just doing marketing' – heck, I made a career and a business out of it for a long time – *but* doing marketing on its own is just a process, a system and a set of actions. If you REALLY want to do your Thing then you need to know what it is first. Then you want to anchor that with a strong Fame Name® that gets remembered and gets you noticed (plus makes you own it). Then tell the story of your Thing so it sticks. Once you've got those pieces in place you have to believe in your Thing. If you're not 'being' your Thing yet, you're still 'doing' it – jump back to Chapter 6 (Nothing is Impossible) until you're ready. When you get your Thing, and you're super-confident about what you do and who you do it for, and you walk around BELIEVING it and owning it, then the marketing is going to be easy.

It's going to be easy

Cue the 80:20 rule. Pareto's principle says that 20% of the effort gives you 80% of the results. Just 20% of your clients and marketing bring you 80% of your income (in my experience this is accurate, by the way). And look – out of the five steps to Being a Business Celebrity this is the last 20%. It will give you 80% of the results but **only** if you've done 80% of the preparation first…

In the old days

When I 'just' did marketing I jumped straight into the spotlight stuff. After all, that's what I was paid to do – marketing and nothing else. But like anything worth doing well, the key is in the preparation…

It's like decorating

If you woke up one morning and thought 'this room needs a makeover', then you could go ahead and do it. A quick trip to the DIY store and you can come home with pots of paint or reams of wallpaper and get stuck in. Start slapping that paint on the walls or splashing on the wallpaper paste like a person possessed. And it's true – you could change the look of a room really fast. Maybe in a morning. It would probably be a bit of a mess though... because to get a great result you need to invest in preparation.

You might want to start out RIGHT at the beginning. If you're not clear on your Thing, erm I mean the purpose of your room, then it would make sense to get some help with that. Ask an interior designer to help you see what your room is best designed for – is it a study or a lounge? A hobby room or a dining room? Then get help with colours and moods and what's going to work best for you (you might know all this but sometimes you need some expert help with the details and interpretation). Now you know what it's for, you can get it right. The room isn't all things to everyone – it's the perfect room for what you want it for.

Next you need to get the room ready – tidy up, cover up anything important, prepare the walls, maybe strip the old wallpaper or smooth out the lumps and bumps. Then you need to tape off all the skirting boards and light switches, tape over anything you don't want painted (shelves, etc.). And this takes ages... zzzzz. By this point you may even be wondering why you thought about decorating in the first place. Was the old room really so bad? Why have you created all this work for yourself? What were you thinking? Is it really so important that you're in the right room...

But now you're ready to decorate. And guess what? Because you planned and prepared and had everything all set up and ready – it takes no time at all. It's now the perfect room for you. You love it. Life is good...

Get some help

The moral of this little decorating story is to get help if you want a great result. Of course anyone can paint a room, but if you want it done right, and right for you, you might need some help with the plan or the execution of it. Just saying…

A spotlight is round

It's a perfect circle of light that shows you off. And it's a bright light. There's no place to hide, so be ready to be noticed. This is about showing you off in your best light. You need to be ready with your Thing and confident to be it.

It's concentrated

A spotlight isn't designed to light up the entire stage, or sky. A spotlight is designed to provide a concentrated circle of light around its subject. It's for pinpointing and being accurate. That is why the clearer you are on the purpose of and the audience for your Thing the better. Your Thing is NOT for everyone. You know that. But a funny thing happens when it comes to marketing…

Don't go general

If I had a pound for every time I've see this happen… I'd be on my yacht in the Caribbean. ☺ Something funny happens on the way to market. Even if you're super-clear on your Thing – you get that you only work with certain people, there's a Fame Name® with your name on it and you're telling your story – you may start to tell everyone.

Everyone is not your audience

Sage marketing advice will tell you 'if you speak to everyone you speak to no-one'. And that is correct. You are NOT here to be the answer for everyone. Your Thing is your Thing and it's only for the people who need your Thing, in fact only a subset of those – the ones with their hands up! You do NOT want to spend your time trying to 'convince' anyone about your Thing. Especially not people who don't even have the problem that you solve!

Ever get a leaflet through the door for mobility scooters or retirement homes when you're years (decades you hope!) off needing them? Or you have ads for weight loss pop up in your Facebook urging you to lose those extra lbs when you're the same dress size you've been since you were 13 (*smug moment*). I get those, and I'm sure you get something just as not needed marketed at you too. What a total waste of effort!

Stick to your Thing

Think spotlight. Think small but bright. Think concentrated, extra strength. Think clear and purposeful. Think star of the stage... If you 'talk to everyone' in your marketing it's the equivalent of having a faint glow of light over a large area – nothing is going to stand out. Instead, if you focus the light in one place it will be hard to miss what's there. Don't think the metaphor of a spotlight is just there for the 'theme' of being a Business Celebrity. It's absolutely there to remind you how to be: *In your Spotlight doing your Thing!*

Communication is all

Some people freak out at the mere mention of the 'M' word (shhh I'll say it quietly – marketing). It's like I've asked them to auction off their granny or sell a family heirloom (which might be the same thing!). All marketing (says she, who is a Member of the Chartered Institute of Marketing) is communication. Marketing (in the world according to me) is saying the right thing, to the right person, at the right time. That is all. The right Thing being the benefit of your

Thing, the right people being those with the problem you solve, and the right time being when they have their hands up saying 'I want to fix this'. I am sure you can talk, and write? Okay, great – then you can communicate, which means you can do marketing.

Clear and confident

This is the most important part of your marketing: clarity and confidence. And if you've worked through your Thing to this point you'll now have this, in spades. You've done the groundwork and now it's just time to show up; to be visible, clearly and confidently telling the right people at the right time (in the right place) about your Thing.

Your Thing is wanted

Do not confuse marketing with selling. Marketing is communicating – it's letting people know you're there. The best musicians in the world don't fill stadiums without marketing. They tell their fans where they are going to be so they can go along and listen to their Thing. *That's* how you fill a stadium. You don't fill a stadium just by being brilliant. The clearer you are on your Thing the easier it will be to connect with the people who need it, and fall on the deaf ears of those who don't.

> **You're not standing on a street corner with a loud hailer (and if you are, please stop!)**

There is no point shouting at everyone. Instead, just speak to the people who need you. Find a way to show them how you can solve their problem. You might make videos, or write, or literally stand in front of them and speak about it, but you're not broadcasting to the world. You're targeting those you talk to, and that's marketing.

Your Thing will only make sense to the people who need it. So talk to them. A lot. Over and over. Show them how it works, why it works, why you do it, tell your story, stick in their heads, show them where to find you... Then you'll be able to sell your Thing by allowing them to visit your store. It's not about dragging people in off the street and forcing them to listen to you and coercing them to buy. Have *you* ever bought anything like that? We don't live in that kind of a world. And why would you want to sell like that anyway? Your Thing is valuable so you don't need to force it on anyone. If anyone needs it they will see its value!

We've done this already

You've already got the perfect tool for this job – your Fame Name®. It has already made you distil your Thing down to a perfect one-liner; a personal headline that will take you anywhere. There was a reason we did this – it makes the rest of your marketing easy. That, and your story as your message. The preparation is done. You know what you stand for, so now it's just time to be counted – to get in your spotlight and get noticed for what you do that's brilliant, *AKA* get famous for your Thing.

Time to find your media Thing

Much as you have the Thing you do that's brilliant, you also have a media Thing – how you *already* (that last word is key) communicate brilliantly. Marketing is communicating and you can already do that. But there is a way you do it best, and this is your media Thing. Again, it's all about the easy (we skip the annoying option here, as it wouldn't make sense to be annoyed in your marketing!).

1000 ways...

There are so many ways you can 'do' your marketing – 1000 ways at least. There are so many types of media and message combinations.

Take care of your important business

My lovely young son is extremely expressive when he takes care of his 'important business' (and yes, I am talking about that important business that happens in the smallest room of the house). His face contorts and there is huffing and puffing until the important business is done. This is the exact same effort I see being put into marketing every day by people *not* doing their media Thing. And I'll be honest, I also see the same result coming out the 'other end' (yes, I am talking about poo!). I am assuming that the last thing you want to do is send out poo to your prospective clients, and I know they certainly don't want to receive it!

Choose wisely

When you find your media Thing you are choosing wisely the media that is easiest for you and, more importantly, does not feel like marketing to you (there is no forcing it out).

Three ways

Which of these do you like the most? (It can be all three if you want!)

The 'creation cave'

Some of us do our best work on our own. I call this being in your creation cave. It's not a literal cave (necessarily) but somewhere you're on your own thinking, writing, recording – or whatever way it is that you do your alone-time communicating. My creation cave is often a train – where I'll write. For other people it's a café, or their office, a shed… who knows? But it's a place where you're communicating on your own, at your best, content you will share later. If you're a writer, or someone who records their ideas, this is you. You don't like distractions and you find your best words when left to your own devices. Your creation cave is where you communicate best.

One to one

Maybe you do your best communicating when there's one other person around. You might be brilliant at conversation or being interviewed. On your own you have your ideas, but when you're one to one they come to life. This is about being clear that you need someone to bounce off, you like feedback and an audience of one to really 'perform' and communicate. If you're asked the right questions you'll come up with epic answers. But if you struggle with the answers… ermmm, this isn't you in flow. If you love to chat, this is you. If you love to be grilled and challenged directly, this is you. Even if you just like to share your writing and get direct feedback, this might be you. It never ceases to amaze me the new answers and new ways of explaining 'Things' that I come up with when I am interviewed. Sometimes you don't know what it is that you have to say until you're asked!

Broadcasting

Do you like an audience? Are you communicating at your best when there is a crowd to entertain? I had no idea this was when I did my best communicating because for years I was too petrified to find out. Now I speak at the drop of a hat, and while I get a little bit nervous I absolutely trust myself that I'll have the right words and I'll say what needs to be said that day to that audience. I'm a far cry from the days when I would read out (yes, word for word) presentations for my MBA while shaking, which seems odd considering my plan was always to be a rock star! What changed for me is that I started to share MY Thing on stage. I used to be afraid of 'getting it wrong' in front of an audience when it wasn't my Thing, so I couldn't be sure I'd 'get it right'. Now that I speak about my Thing there is no way of anyone knowing it's not right (apart from me). And that's a relief, so I relax.

In fact, here's what I've learnt makes you a great speaker:

- energy
- connection
- trust.

If you can manage the energy in a room – and by that I mean be present with your audience – you can give them what they came for. If you can connect with your audience, you're halfway there – and that's everything from eye contact to knowing what stories to tell and how to tell them. And trust? Well that's trust in yourself that you'll stand up there and say absolutely the right thing that you need to. If you ask me what I am going to say 2 minutes before I stand up to speak I honestly can't tell you the exact words in the exact order. Of course I can give you the 'gist' and I have a topic and a structure for my talk, but every single actual word? Who knows! There is definitely no script being read. And that's something I've realised along with finding my Thing – I have something to say and I need to say it. So I actually love to broadcast, because for me the energy in the room gives me even more energy to do my Thing, and that's only ever a good thing! If you've ever seen me speak live you'll know this. And while you might think 'how does she remember all that?' don't worry; I don't – I just trust the right words will come. And they do.

So, do you like an audience? Make sure you shoot video, get speaking gigs and get on TV if you do, then you'll be communicating your Thing the best way you know how.

Finding your media Thing makes your Thing sing

Trying to force a square peg through a round hole is never a good idea. Yes of course it will fit if you bash it hard enough, but that's going to take a whole lot of effort. And the whole point of doing your Thing is that it's easy. Take the easy route with your media Thing too. Then your marketing (shh, whisper it) is just an extension of how you already like to communicate. You're not 'learning' something new, you're not pushing something out and it's going to work for you, as it's how you already like to do things. After all, you only want to sing the songs you like…

Translate it

Take your media Thing and translate it into your marketing. Every type of communication will have its matching marketing; there is no way of communicating that can't be turned into marketing.

If you like to hang out in your creation cave – have a blog, write for other people, write articles, author a book, write a script, be a poet. I don't know which of these is right for you, but they can all work as marketing.

If you like to communicate one to one then get interviewed! Record audio interviews, film them, transcribe them. Have conversations turned into copy. Work out what it is that you say when you're one to one and turn that into your marketing.

Broadcaster? Well this one's much more obvious! Get on TV or start a YouTube channel or podcast, star on a radio show, hire an agent. Do what you need to do to get in front of a big audience (even if you have to start your own channel). This is marketing that will work for you!

Use a checklist

If you want an actual checklist you can grab one on this book's website. But you can draw up your own easily too. Write down all the marketing you've been thinking of doing or are doing right now, and tick what is you REALLY doing your media Thing. There's a lot to choose from, so I'll give you some starters for 10.

But first...

Know who you are talking to. I have two words for you here: the first is 'Ideal' and the second is 'Client'. I have made this point already when I said you *only* want to talk to people with their *hands up*. That's who those 'hands-up' people are – Ideal Clients. They are people who HAVE the problem you solve with your Thing AND they want to DO SOMETHING about it. They have their hands up for help. And you can help them.

When you know who you're talking to you'll get results (and by results I mean sales for you, too, not just results for the people who get your Thing). So your Ideal Clients are those people who resonate with your Fame Name®, they are the people who sit up and take notice when you tell your story, and they are who you're 'talking to' (communicating with) when you do your marketing.

Don't worry about the others

When you focus on your Ideal Clients you don't need to worry about the others. You're not marketing to the others – only to those people with their hands up. Always remember this (especially when you ask 'friends' for feedback!)… What happens when you focus on your Ideal Clients is that all the people around who actually want to be your Ideal Clients also want to work with you. They show up. But if you try to talk to all the other people, you won't have enough time.

The more focused you become, the more people you attract because people want to be the people you are focused on. So even if you think you need to talk to 'everyone' (we mentioned that panic), don't. The others don't want what you've got so why tell them about it? Why waste your wonderful energy?

Where are they then?

These 'hands-up' people aren't listed in the phone directory under 'H' (or 'U' for that matter). They don't all belong to a special 'I've got my hands up for you club'. But you can still find them as easily as if they were.

When I say 'where does your Ideal Client hang out?' I mean what media do they see? What are you going to find them reading/watching/listening to? You need to know where they hang out – literally in some cases – because that's where you're going to show up too, in your spotlight. Right words, right time, right place. Let me count the ways… For each of the following ideas, make a note of how you feel about them – would you be forcing them out if you did them? Choosing your spotlight is practical *and* emotional (that's why we know it will work – because you'll WANT to do it).

Of course they have to be there

Quick note on the media thing Thing

Remember that your Ideal Clients do have to be paying attention to the media you choose. I appreciate you might have a few media things on your list that you love *but* if your market doesn't listen to/see/read/watch some of the ones you've chosen then **don't do them!**

I'd like to think I didn't have to point this out (it being rather obvious!) but you'd be surprised. I've seen smart people do some silly things before. ☺

The power of 3×3

Here's a thing you can do. Take three different 'reactions' to media things and then (when you've worked your way through the checklist) pick out the three most exciting/enticing/easy. This is how I do marketing plans. And here are the three reactions:

- Love it
- Nervous
- Not for me.

'Love it' I'm guessing is pretty self-explanatory: you'd do it all day long, you have no problem with it, you love it. 'Nervous' and 'Not for me' I need to explain a little more because being nervous about something is very, very different from something not being right for you. The whole premise behind stepping into your spotlight is that there's the 'stepping into' part of it and some nervous energy usually goes along with that! That is exactly why I don't do any spotlight-getting-into until we've been through the 'nothing is impossible'. There is method in my madness!

So, if you're nervous about stepping into the spotlight that's fine. That's kind of expected, if I'm honest, because if you weren't a little nervous about it you'd probably be in your spotlight already. You wouldn't be reading this book to find your Thing as you'd already be on it, doing it, smashing it, top of the charts (etc.)!

'Nervous' does not equal 'not doing'

I know I promised that your marketing was going to be easy and right now you might be thinking 'well, I'm sorry, you've just contradicted yourself there because you said I'm going to be scared and nervous and it's not going to be easy'. Er, yes and you would be right. But it's just for a moment. There will be a moment when you have to step up to your spotlight, but once you've done it, then it's easy. So I reckon I've wriggled my way out of that one, right?

It's not you...

Just like you know when you're not doing your Thing thing (the uniform goes on, everything is hard work) you'll know when something isn't your media Thing when you have an adverse reaction to it (usually a pretty strong one!). Watch out for nerves clouding your judgement though – you might think 'Uh! I couldn't possibly stand on stage and talk about my Thing' or 'I couldn't possibly go on the radio "I couldn't possibly write an article for that magazine" I can't, I can't, I can't…' That's nerves … if you're feeling nervous about it, that is actually a sign that you should do it. But if you're feeling 'Ooh, no, that's not sitting right with me, that's not who I am, that's not me in my flow', that's when you don't do it. It's not your media Thing when you feel like that. If you don't enjoy it, don't do it, don't force it!

You won't miss out

There are tons of alternative media things, so don't worry that you're blocking people reaching you. I can't think of anyone who only looks at one type of media ever! So don't panic that you're not going to catch people's attention. It's just really important right now to focus on the media things that you already love and some of the things that you're nervous about.

Linda – The Why Parent – got really clear on her media Thing, quickly working it out to be a combination of one to one and broadcasting. She loves dialogue with parents so they can trust her as a person, they can see she is authentic and passionate about what she does. And this isn't all that surprising when you know Linda's background is as a teacher and psychologist and parent herself, which is all about connection and understanding people when you're face to face with them.

Count to three

Once you've worked out all your possible media things, then count to three. Pick ONLY the three that you love the most and do those. Nothing else. Just three… That's the easiest way to organise your marketing so it won't overwhelm you. Simply pick three, and do them brilliantly of course!

A spotlight is bright

The more focus you have on your Thing and your media Thing, the brighter it will shine. If you only have three types of marketing to focus on I'm betting they'll work better for you than 10 or 20 or 50 (as your energy won't be scattered). Your Thing is about getting results for people and my Thing is to get YOU results for doing your Thing (it gets confusing, I know – all these Things). So the more focused you are on your Thing the better. Don't scatter your energy all over the show doing every type of marketing that crosses your path. If people can't see you because you're not in a bright focused beam of light, then you're not going to reach all the people you can. Too many different marketing media and you've got your dimmer switch on.

Let's look at the list...

Let's go through the big list that I've got here of media things. The list is split into two main types – offline and online. Offline is everything that isn't online, so traditional marketing, print media, live audiences, etc. Online is anything Web-related, anything that people will access online.

About your website

I'm going to talk in a bit more detail about websites and Web presence in a minute, but there's no escaping it these days; you do need a focal point on the Web. This *doesn't* have to be an all-singing, all-dancing website however. Your focal point online can be a Facebook page. It can be a landing page (a one-page website). It can be a blog, a YouTube channel or an App. But it has to be there. You must have something online so that when people Google (or use any other search engine) your Fame Name®, your actual name, your business or your Thing, you will be found. You need to have something online that you can point people to where they can find you. So don't panic if you haven't got a website, do panic if you haven't got a focal point!

Offline media things

Speak to people on the phone

Old school! Talking to real people? On a phone (maybe even a landline!)? I'll be asking you to fax people next (I won't really…). Yes this is marketing – one-to-one calls to people, or phoning people from your list. It might be having strategy calls, it might be just picking up the phone and introducing yourself to people, or following up from networking or other events. Your marketing isn't just about your potential clients either – it's also about suppliers and partners, people who promote you and anyone who's going to help you be visible in your market. And they all have a phone number – so dial it!

> ## Sidetrack
>
> While knowing who your Ideal Clients are is super-important, it's also important to know who else to talk to who can get you in front of them. Always **think around the edges**. Always be thinking 'who else knows or has contact with or could put me in front of my Ideal Clients?' Being visible to partners or suppliers helps a lot with getting famous for your Thing.

PR

Here I mean public relations in the traditional sense of getting column inches, getting in print, getting in magazines, getting in newspapers, or getting radio air time or TV gigs. PR means getting noticed by the media by putting yourself out there, by sending out press releases, by speaking to editors and producers. Tell them your story – and the great news is you've got all this stuff ready. You've got your Fame Name®, you know why you're different, you've got your PSP so away you go. Tell them why the world needs your Thing. It works especially well when you can tie it in with topical events already 'in the news'.

Direct mail

Being a 'mature' marketer (i.e., old!) I've had my share of envelope-stuffing days when the mailing machine broke down, but direct mail still works and actually the irony is that direct mail probably works even better now, because not everyone's doing it. I love getting hand-written cards through the post or something quirky in a parcel. It gets my attention. And if what is delivered can help me, then I pay serious attention. What can you send by mail that shows off your Thing? Have a think then get to the Post Office!

Networking

Meeting people 'for real' is great marketing – not to mention it's a fabulous way to test out your stories and Fame Name® for stickiness. Do make sure they are your Ideal Clients though, before you take on board all the feedback you might get while networking. Just a little warning here – we're not concerned with 'the others' who might be in the room. A fast-track way to get despondent about your Thing is to talk to a room full of people who don't have their hands up, as of course they don't want or need your Thing so they aren't ever going to be excited about it! The magic of networking lies in the follow-up, so don't think showing up will magically get you clients. You need to have conversations too – marketing is communication after all.

Speaking

You can't get a much more literal interpretation of getting into your spotlight than hopping on a stage. Speaking can come in all shapes and sizes – it can be standing up at that networking group, or inviting six people to a small workshop; it can be a stadium or a theatre too of course! And if speaking gets a tick in your 'Nervous' category, just remember – if it's you connecting direct with your Ideal Clients and you being able to communicate in your flow then it's a really good, super-direct, media thing. I've never failed to get a client from speaking – either then and there in the room directly or afterwards. You just never know who is listening, but you do know they are getting to see you do your Thing right that minute and if it's something they need they'll want to buy it, so let them.

Face to face

Obviously it's a little labour intensive having conversations one person at a time, but it's still marketing if you're sharing your Thing. If you're starting out with your Thing then absolutely do build up relationships one by one. If what you're building up is strong and powerful then your spotlight's only going to get bigger, because those people are going to make referrals. Acorns grow into oak trees and great one-to-one conversations grow into great business.

Radio

Okay, this is a sneaky one really as there are tons of online radio stations now which makes it a lot easier to get on the airwaves; and these stations are often more targeted, with radio shows for really niched and specific audiences. So that's a cross-platform fabulous media thing I really encourage you to use as it will enable you to reach the 'hands-up' people who need your Thing.

Events

You can go to other people's events and be visible as a participant or an audience member or, if you're feeling bold, a sponsor (or a speaker of course!). You can also host your own events. Nothing says 'I know what I'm talking about' like saying 'I'm having an event'. Go on… you can do it!

TV

Hey, why not? It's just another type of media. See who you can connect to, or email and tweet with producers and editors. If they are looking for your Thing then make sure they find you! Sometimes you can get on TV (and this works for other types of media too) by doing other things, like blogging or videos or speaking. You may be surprised who will notice you. You can also start your own TV show. It's called a YouTube channel or V-log (video blog), but now I'm creeping into online media things… more on those in a minute.

Ads

Print ads, posters, fliers, anything that's traditional media and probably involves paper can work to get you famous. All the usual rules and 'where is your Ideal Client?' conditions apply. And *have a call to action…* Do not under any circumstances have a 'pretty' ad that looks good but tells us nothing about your Thing and why we need to contact you now. You're not after brand awareness, you're after customers! So ask for action in your ad.

Write a book

Now obviously I cannot say this is a bad idea. However, it can also be a very nice distraction from doing your Thing. This is absolutely NOT where you start with your marketing. My advice would always be to only write a book if you can sustain your day-to-day marketing at the same time, because it takes a lot of time and effort. Do not disappear into your creation cave and emerge months later wondering where your business went. Only write a book when the media things you are doing are *already working* (or be prepared for no clients, it's up to you!). And actually, it's much, much better for you to wait until you have what publishers call a 'platform' (people who already love you and your Thing) because then it makes your book launch super-easy. When you've used *your* media Thing to generate a lovely list of people with their hands up you'll have an audience to launch your book to straight away.

Pick something you can start tomorrow

I've already taken you through some ideas for offline media things, and online is coming up. But whatever ticks you're ticking (and there are those three categories of 'Love', 'Nervous' and 'Not for me'), don't pick the hard ones. Don't choose media things that mean you have to disappear for days/months/years to learn how to do them and 'get them right' first. We need your Thing NOW, so best to have a way of us seeing your Thing right now too.

Online media things

Your website

Obviously, your website is a great media thing to have – whether this is a 'brochure' website just telling us about you and your Thing, or a fully interactive selling machine, a website is a very good idea.

On the cover of a magazine

Imagine the homepage of your website as the front cover of a magazine. You need a great big hero shot image – on a magazine that would be the cover shot – and then you work with headlines that show people all the different items that are included. In a magazine these would be articles, on your website they are sign-posts to read more on your site. Everything someone needs to know to make a decision about whether to buy that magazine or not is on the front cover. So your website needs to be the same – everything someone needs to know to decide if your Thing will help them or not needs to be on the homepage. If you read a magazine, often you read the first paragraph and think 'Okay, yup, that article's interesting, I'll carry on reading that' – so structure your website in a similar way: give people something – enough to know if they want to read more or not about your Thing – and then give them the opportunity to read more. After that, signpost them to other useful things. Have your website 100% tuned into WII FM (What's In It For Me?). And *always* let people sign up for something that will help them on the first step of getting your answer to the Thing-based problem so you can trade it for an email address and keep in touch. You need to know who has their hands up for REAL.

Quick! Tell me the Thing!

Your Thing needs to be all over you website. *All over it…* At every turn there you are again telling us about your Thing, giving us examples, sharing stories about it, showcasing testimonials about how your Thing really works. Thing Thing Thing. This is *your space* online so make it all about YOU and your Thing! The site doesn't have to be all bells and whistles, but make sure it captures attention and clearly states who it's for (and who it's not for), what you can do for people and why you're the best person to do it. Use it to show off your Thing.

Social media

This can of course be a huge distraction… a marvellous one for me, I'll admit (I love Facebook a little too much!). That said, it can also be immensely powerful for getting you into your spotlight and a brilliant media thing. Do not underestimate the power of social media – I am a huge, huge fan. I've certainly reached people and got clients from it directly, no question about it. The possibilities that you have now to connect with people so quickly and so directly are just huge, thanks to social media. But it can be a little bit of a time black hole, so you do have to watch out for that (again, ahem).

So, knowing your Thing, being clear and confident about it, and absolutely knowing who your hands-up people are is super-important. I'm not saying ONLY connect with those people. Absolutely not. At the end of the day, it's *social* media and you should use it in a sociable way but be clear about who you work with and the social connections will do their thing for you. For me, the 'big three' of social media (what is it about threes and media things?!) are Facebook, LinkedIn and Twitter; different people live – or hang out – on each.

In a nutshell, LinkedIn is great for 'business' and business-to-business conversations. If your hands-up people are corporate or work 'in business' this is your playground. If you're after solopreneurs and people doing all sorts of things, then Facebook is where you need to be spending more time. Twitter covers everyone – and is especially good for journalist stalking (!) and connecting 'above your station'. I personally find 140 characters a challenge ☺ but it's a great way to get your Thing out into the world. Social media makes marketing a level playing field, so go knock it out of the park!

Don't let it take over…

Whichever media things you choose, don't let them take over your life. The whole point of finding ways to communicate that you love and can do easily is that you get them done. THEN you can move on and do your Thing. You are not paid to do marketing (unless your Thing IS marketing!), you are paid when you do your Thing – so get as much bang for your buck as you can, with marketing that pays you back.

Getting found easily online

Being in the spotlight of Google and other search engines is going to come as a result of great search engine optimisation (SEO) or pay-per-click advertising (like Google ads) if you want to be found when people type in a 'search term'. Just something to bear in mind, and ask an online expert about, and perhaps do some research on if you want to go deeper into keyword searches to get you famous. But referrals are important too. So if you're being talked about (and let's face it, with that Fame Name® it's pretty likely!) you want to make sure you're signposting yourself well online so that you're found. I'm not going to get technical here, but suffice to say: make sure you can be found easily online for your Fame Name®, your story, your message, your philosophy and more. Leave digital footprints wherever you know your Ideal Clients may be too and send them over to your website/blog/YouTube channel. Have an online journey that you can take people on so they get to really 'see' you doing your Thing.

Blogging and vlogging

Package up your Thing into blog posts (words) or videos (vlogs) and post them online in these special types of website that search engines love. And if you're hosting your videos online remember that YouTube is the second biggest search engine after Google and many a 'How To' search happens there (valuable when you want to get noticed for your Thing).

Guest blogging, interviews and other people's lists

Yes, I'm putting a few media things together now (otherwise this list is going to get *very* long). But think about where you can show up that isn't your domain online. Who else is talking to your hands-up people already? Demonstrate that you know your Thing, demonstrate that you know what you're talking about and go and offer to guest blog or write an article for someone else. Chances are your Thing is the thing their people need right before or right after their Thing…

It's very easy to show up everywhere your Ideal Clients are online. Let's be honest, you can't be speaking in 100 different places on the same day to groups of your hands-up clients, but you can certainly show up in 100 different places online in the same day where they are hanging out – and that's really what you're aiming for in order to get famous fast.

Email your peeps!

Don't forget that we all email… a lot! While you might need a little time to build up your own list of email addresses, there are some lovely people out there with email lists that have your hands-up people on them already. So ask if you can write to them to share a story, talk about your Thing. Then offer them something of value so they will join your list and then you can email them some more about your Thing (HELPFUL emails usually work best here, not salesy ones). Content is king in the land of the Internet so show off and showcase your Thing, don't sell it – that will happen automatically if you're doing a good job in your spotlight. Remember, you can give away a lot of information and charge for the action.

I know no-one!

If you're sat there thinking 'I know no one, I have no clue where to find these mythical Ideal Client creatures' then go find people who already know them. It's the quickest and easiest way to share your Thing with an audience ready to receive you. Smart business owners are looking for useful content to share with their clients and potential clients all the time, or speakers for their events, or guests on their radio shows/blogs/websites. People are always looking to add value to what they can give their own clients and crowd, and so if you can show up to add that value with your Thing then it's fantastic, everyone's happy, it's a win/win.

Joint ventures rock

Joint ventures are a great marketing strategy, and they can work really, really well. No point reinventing the wheel if somewhere it's already turning.

What did you tick?

Back to the list of media things. What did you tick? How are you going to go out tomorrow and tell your hands-up people about your Thing? Yes tomorrow. (Yes you can… start now, or as soon as you've finished this book!)

Turn it up to 11

I'm talking about amplification! Once you've picked out your three media things, get them working, then work on amplifying them. See how what you're already doing can be repositioned, tweaked or changed a little bit or adapted to be something else. There's always the next notch up on the dial that you can take those media things too. A louder volume, a bigger audience. For example, if you're writing blog posts, those can become articles; if you've made some great videos, look at how you can turn them into PR. Look at where you're totally rocking your communication and get louder!

Er, is that it?

Yes, that's it. More than 20 years of marketing experience in a nutshell: do three media things and do them really well. That's what works. And I see it work over and over again! It is that easy…

- Show up.
- Do your Thing.
- Be your Fame Name®.
- Tell your story.
- Own your spotlight (all the time knowing nothing is impossible).

Make waves

Here's how you want to roll… You want to have a constantly rolling wave of marketing activity happening to show off you and your Thing. I am talking every day/week/month you are doing something so you don't disappear off the radar of your 'hands-up' market. The opposite situation to this is a tidal marketing wave. I know I've been on the receiving end of these.

Ever heard nothing from a company or business for a while then all of a sudden they're everywhere? Emails upon emails in your inbox from them, their friends, anyone else who knows them, all promoting their Thing like crazy. They are everywhere you turn online and letters are coming through your door. You are literally drowning in their marketing! That wave is way too scary to surf! And just as quickly as it reared up, the wave has crashed onto the shore and it's gone. They disappear again until they have something else to sell!

Instead, keep it simple, keep it moving, roll your wave on and on so it's a good one to surf. That's why I say do three media things. Your three media things power your wave, that's what keeps it rolling. Then, when you want a little more attention – maybe you've got an offer you want to make or a launch you want to share – you only need to ramp it up a notch (not a mile) to make us notice. We're already used to seeing you and hearing from you (with useful content too) so when you have something extra for us we're all ears and we see it. We also don't see you crash and burn afterwards either. We carry on hearing from you whether we take you up on your offer this time or not. Surfing a rolling wave is way cooler. And we want to be the cool kids doing our Thing, right?

Here's what the marketing wave looks like (the tidal wave is that spiky one).

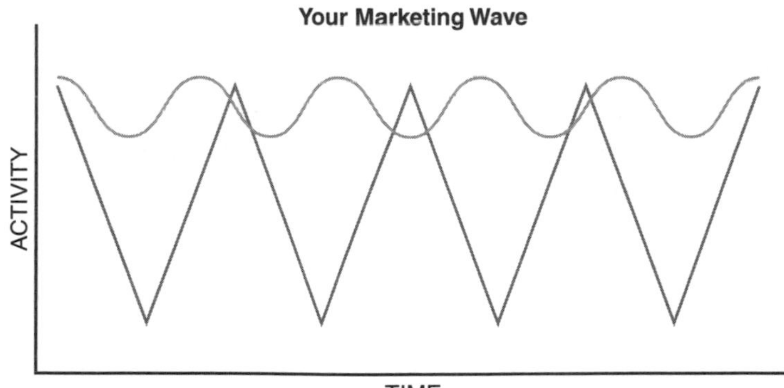

Ride the merry-go-round

Consistently and confidently doing your Thing and your media Thing is a fun ride people want to stay on. It's not a roller coaster, and it's not a ghost train either. It's a perfectly nice, but not scary for anyone, carousel ride. It's up and down, round and round, and people that like it will stay on until they are ready to get off. And when they get off it's to buy from you. This is another way of looking at the marketing wave. Make your media things a nice merry-go-round ride of information and ideas and education and entertainment that people stay on until they are ready to get off and do something.

Information versus action

You can give away a LOT of information. All of it, in fact. I can give away everything I know and I'll still have clients who will pay me for the ACTION. Don't hold back on your marketing. Use your media things to tell us everything you know about your Thing. It won't matter. We'll still buy action-taking and the 'real work' from you.

The Internet is one giant WiKi of information… there's know-how until the cows come home. It won't stop you being hired because most people know DIY is false economy. So do what you want with your media things. Tell the whole world about your Thing and how it works. Share all the information you have. You'll still get action-takers who want to buy.

GET BUSINESS FAMOUS

Do your Thing so I can do mine

When you show up with your Fame Name® on your T-shirt, standing in your spotlight confidently showing us the clear Thing that you do, I know who you are. I know who I am because I'm wearing my T-shirt too. And if you have a Thing that helps me, I am going to want to talk to you. Don't try to do everything – this will only divert your time, energy and attention away from doing YOUR THING.

Be valued

For me it makes sense that when you find your Thing you turn that into a business. And then you get business famous for it. That whole 'sitting at home on your own being amazing' doesn't go down all that well with me, as you know... because you need to be valued. Your Thing is valuable; it needs to be done. You need to be doing it. And quite rightly you shouldn't have to do it for free.

It's not free

I can rant about this for days. I know you find your Thing easy. I know you would do your Thing all day long for nothing just because you love it. But that isn't going to allow you to do it as much or as often as you'd like to (or as often or as much as the people with their hands up would like you to). Unless you're already a billionaire and can give up all your time for charitable Thinging causes (and bravo you if that is the case) then you need to get paid. And that's the point of getting business famous for your Thing, because you also don't want to waste all your time selling.

Let them come to you

When you get business famous for your Thing people come to you. With their hands in the air! You are stood in your spotlight – visible for your Thing – and you attract attention.

Being attractive

You want to get the flow of marketing moving towards you. Being business famous magnetises you so you are followed, people are coming TO you, not you having to chase them. You reverse the polarity. This is why taking your time on the 80% of foundation building of Being a Business Celebrity really *really* works. Once you have that clarity on your Thing, you can get the powerful Fame Name® that makes you memorable. Then tell your story and make it as sticky as you can. Put that story jam everywhere so you leave a trail of sticky footprints leading back to you and your Thing. Own it completely, think it and believe it. Then pick out your media things, surf the marketing wave and watch people notice you in your spotlight. This is what getting business famous looks like… it might not be a queue around the block when you start, but you'll be building an audience that wants your Thing.

This is everything

- You doing your Thing is such a gift.
- It's a gift for you (you'll love it, trust me).
- It's a gift to me (as that's my Thing having its impact).
- And it's a gift to everyone else – hands up or otherwise.

Obviously to the people who are waiting for you to show up with your Thing, it's perfect – they now have the answer to their problem, a cure for their pain. And for everyone else – well, we're all connected so that pebble you threw in the pond with your Thing will ripple out to everyone somehow (even though you didn't aim for them). Rather a utopian view I agree, but that's how I see it. Which is why I hope you do it. I really hope you find your Thing. And more importantly, you then go and do it. Give me a shout if you need a hand.

With much Thinging love…

Lucy x

MORE RESOURCES

This book has it's own website www.FindYourThingBook.com where I've gathered together a bunch of gorgeous goodies for you.

Because Finding your Thing is one thing and Doing your Thing is entirely another – and you might need a hand with both!

At www.FindYourThingBook.com you'll find (for free I must add)…

- Thing related videos
- A Fame Name® class
- Interviews with people doing their Thing
- Checklists and worksheets (the ones I mentioned already in the book and some extras too – so you can tick off and work Things out)
- Access to my latest thoughts (that will be a blog then!)

…along with whatever else I think is a good goodie for you to have!

You'll also be able to see when I'm next hosting a live online class or an 'in real life' event (I do like to go on tour).

And if you fancy the idea of getting some help with your Thing (finding it, getting famous for it, or both) you'll be able to see options and opportunities to do that too.

www.FindYourThingBook.com

It's where the Thing thing is at!

ABOUT THE AUTHOR

Lucy Whittington works with clients worldwide to Find their Thing and Get Famous for it. She launched www.BeingABusinessCelebrity.com after having run an 'ordinary' marketing consultancy (since 2005).

After realising her ambition to be a rock star was not quite working out (how many pop princesses do you know with an Economics degree?), she did the next best thing and got 'good' at marketing, working in organisations ranging from start-ups to International Plcs. Eventually, after getting overqualified with an MBA, Lucy realised that her 'Thing' was finding other people's Thing and turning that into a great business they loved.

Lucy lives at the seaside – which she will definitely mention without being prompted – with her husband (the colouring-in department) and their 2 small people. When not on the school run or at the beach, she can be found working one to one with VIP clients (often on a yacht) hosting a monthly Business Club, running her own live events or on Skype to all corners of the globe Thinging with fabulous people online.

Lucy loves to talk Things – and loves being on stage, on radio, in podcasts, webinars and other interviews on the topic of Thing finding and Being a Business Celebrity. You'll find her at events ranging from entrepreneur to wealth summits to business and networking groups with audiences ranging from 30-300 people (live) and many more online. Good luck shutting her up if you're not doing your Thing yet.

She has been featured on the BBC and in The Guardian, The Sun, Red, The Marketing Donut, and Top Sante.

If you ever want to know what's going on inside Lucy's head then read her blog www.LucyLovesBusiness.com – she has opinions on most things (and Things!).